CISTERCIAN STUDIES SERIES: NUMBER TWO HUNDRED

Grimlaicus
Rule for Solitaries

D1548284

CISTERCIAN STUDIES SERIES: NUMBER TWO HUNDRED

Grimlaicus

Rule for Solitaries

Translated with Introduction and Notes by
Andrew Thornton, OSB

α

Cistercian Publications
www.cistercianpublications.org

LITURGICAL PRESS
Collegeville, Minnesota
www.litpress.org

A Cistercian Publications title published by Liturgical Press

Cistercian Publications
Editorial Offices
Abbey of Gethsemani
3642 Monks Road
Trappist, Kentucky 40051
www.cistercianpublications.org

2	3	4	5	6	7	8	9

Library of Congress Cataloging-in-Publication Data

Grimlaicus, fl. 900.
    [Regula solitariorum. English]
    Grimlaicus : rule for solitaries / translated with introduction and notes by Andrew Thornton.
      p. cm. — (Cistercian studies series ; 200)
    "This volume presents the first English translation of the Regula solitariorum of Grimlaicus"—Introd.
    Includes bibliographical references and indexes.
    ISBN 978-0-87907-200-1 — ISBN 978-0-87907-830-0 (e-book)
     1. Monasticism and religious orders—Rules. 2. Cenobites.
I. Thornton, Andrew L., 1946– II. Title. III. Title: Rule for solitaries.

BX2436.5.G75E5 2011
255'.0109409021—dc22

                                2010030877

Contents

Abbreviations

CC	*Corpus Christianorum: series latina.* Brepols: Turnhout.
CCCM	*Corpus Christianorum: continuatio mediaevalis.* Brepols: Turnhout.
Defensor	*Defensor Locociagensis monachi Scintillarum Liber.* PL 88:597–718. See also: *Defensoris Locogiacensis monachi Liber Scintillarum,* ed. D. Henricus Rochais, O.S.B. CC vol. 117. Turnhout: Brepols, 1957. Since chapter 32 of this critical edition is not in PL, the chapter numbers thereafter are higher by one.
Ep(p)	*Epistula/ae*
MGH	*Monumenta Germaniae Historica*
PL	*Patrologia Latina,* ed. J-P. Migne.
RB	The Rule of Saint Benedict
SCh	*Sources Chrétiennes. Les Éditions du Cerf:* Paris.

Introduction[1]

This volume presents the first English translation of the *Regula solitariorum* of Grimlaicus, the first rule for people who live as cenobitic solitaries, that is, who live enclosed in a solitary area but within the context of a monastic community.[2]

There are a number of reasons for introducing Grimlaicus to those who read English. First, Grimlaicus' rule is far more than a list of regulations meant to govern an extreme form of the ascetical life. It contains a balanced theology of the contemplative life and a rationale for living this life in a way that fosters spiritual, psychological, and physical health. Second, Grimlaicus' rule is a splendid witness to the vitality of the patristic and monastic tradition between the Carolingian reform and the flowering of Cluniac and Cistercian monasticism. Grimlaicus is thoroughly familiar with the Rule of Saint Benedict and uses it as the foundation for a style of life quite different from that for which the Rule was intended. Third, through the rule of Grimlaicus, we meet its author. He acts as a conduit for a great tradition that reaches back to New Testament

---

[1] Portions of this introduction appeared as an article in the *American Benedictine Review*, 59, no. 2 (June 2008): 198–212. This material is used here by permission of the *American Benedictine Review*.

[2] This translation uses the Latin text of *Grimlaici presbyteri regula solitariorum* in *Codex Regularum Monasticarum et Canonicarum*, ed. Lucas Holstenius, vol. 1, critico-historical notes by Marianus Brockie (Augsburg: Adam & Veith, 1759), 291–344. (1957 repr. Vienna: Akademische Druck und Verlagsanstalt). Holstenius' edition is reprinted in PL 103:574–664.

times, yet he also intends that readers hear his own voice, the voice of a man conscious of his fallibility yet confident in his authority; moderate and realistic in assessing situations and persons yet uncompromising in his pursuit of ideals; deeply troubled at laxity and abuses yet eager to have others discover the joy he has found.

Because Grimlaicus' rule has a clear message framed in straightforward language, it needs no lengthy introduction. Consequently these remarks simply provide some biographical, historical, and literary context.

The Author

In the opening lines of his preface, the author of the *Regula solitariorum* says that he is writing the rule at the request of one Grimlaicus and that he himself also has that name. Who was this person, and where and when did he live?

Brockie[3] notes that Mabillon, in his *Annalibus Benedictinis*, mentions a certain Grimlaicus who lived around the year 900 and was a close associate of Pope Formosus and a worthy bishop. Mabillon suggests that this man could have been either the author of the rule or the one to whom it was dedicated. Mabillon also thought that Grimlaicus might have originally come from Rheims, since the history of that city shows a Grimlaicus, a priest, toward the end of the ninth century.[4] As Gougaud points out, however, the name was a common one.

Brockie thought that Grimlaicus lived at Metz or nearby.[5] Metz seems a likely location, since Grimlaicus several times praises Arnulf, bishop of Metz (d. 640)[6] and twice cites the *Rule for Canons* of Amalarius of Metz (d. 850).[7] Grimlaicus' remarks in the prologue to his rule, as well as his complete familiarity with the physical and

---

[3] Holstenius-Brockie, 292.

[4] L. Gougaud, OSB, "Étude sur la réclusion religieuse," *Revue Mabillon* 8 (1923): 26–39 and 77–102.

[5] Holstenius-Brockie, 292.

[6] Chaps. 1 and 63.

[7] Chap. 41.

spiritual circumstances of the life of an *inclusus*, make it clear that
he had lived such a life himself for a good while.

Just as clear is
Grimlaicus' remarkable familiarity with the Rule of Benedict, now
citing it nearly verbatim, now modifying it to fit the situation of
enclosed solitaries, but always drawing on its good sense, moderation, and adaptability.[8] This sort of familiarity was surely the fruit
of years lived in a community that observed Benedict's Rule. Thus
Grégoire's suggestion that Grimlaicus might have been associated
with the monastery of Gorze in the diocese of Metz seems reasonable.[9] Karl Suso Frank agrees with this line of reasoning, further
conjecturing that Grimlaicus may have written his rule after the
time of Robert, bishop of Metz and abbot of Gorze, who died in
917.[10]

Even though Frank admits that "the author has eluded all attempts to identify him,"[11] this series of informed guesses leads us
to assume that Grimlaicus was a monk who lived around the year
900, very likely at Gorze or, at any rate, in or near Metz.

Enclosed Solitaries before Grimlaicus

In order to appreciate the unique features of Grimlaicus' rule,
it would be well to get some idea of how solitaries who dwelled
within monastic communities lived in late Roman and early medieval times.[12] Against what historical background did Grimlaicus

---

[8] Not counting the liturgical and disciplinary codes of RB (chaps. 8–15 and
23–28), Grimlaicus cites or refers to roughly 35% of the text of Benedict's Rule.

[9] Réginald Grégoire, "Grimlaic," in *Dictionnaire de spiritualité acétique et
mystique*, M. Viller et al., (Paris: Beauchesne, 1967), vol. 6, cols. 1042–43.

[10] Karl Suso Frank, "Grimlaicus, 'Regula solitariorum,'" in *Vita Religiosa im
Mittelalter: Festschrift für Kaspar Elm*, ed. F. J. Felten and N. Jaspert, 21–35 (Berlin:
Duncker & Humbolt, 1999), 22.

[11] Ibid., 21.

[12] Needless to say, the much larger category of solitaries who lived apart, often
in the wasteland or in tombs, cannot be dealt with here. The list of primary sources
is enormous: the lives of the fathers and mothers of the deserts of Egypt, Palestine,
Syria and Cappadocia, as well as the lives of ascetics in the West, including Sulpicius
Severus' life of Saint Martin and Gregory the Great's life of Saint Benedict.

write? What sorts of usages or abuses might his rule have been addressing?

In the West, the first legislation for solitaries who live within a monastery occurs in the *acta* of the local council of Vannes, which took place between 461 and 491.

> The following is to be observed concerning monks: they are not to be permitted to withdraw from the community into solitary cells, except in the case of those who have been proven after prolonged labors or [the case in which], because of the needs imposed by weakness, the rigor of the rule is relaxed by abbots. This is to be done such that they remain within the enclosure of the monastery yet are permitted to have separate cells under the abbot's authority.[13]

This very early legislation contains some elements that will be prominent in Grimlaicus' rule: only after prolonged testing are monks allowed to live as solitaries; even then the cells are to be inside the enclosure, and the enclosed monks are to remain under the abbot's authority. Yet the legislation of Vannes does not seem to be addressing precisely the sort of life later envisaged by Grimlaicus. There is no mention of permanent reclusion or of the cell's being sealed. If there were arrangements for food and access to the Divine Office and Mass, they are not mentioned. In fact, the council recognizes that certain monks who may dwell in solitary cells are those for whom the strictness of the common rule has to be mitigated.

The works of Gregory of Tours,[14] who wrote a century after the Council of Vannes, fairly burst with solitaries. Gregory was writing about the Merovingian domain, chiefly Tours and its environs, in the latter half of the sixth century. Even at several centuries' remove, the glimpses he gives of solitaries, especially those who lived in the midst of monastic groups, can perhaps give some idea of the background against which Grimlaicus, shortly after the year 900, for-

---

[13] "*Concilium Veneticum*," in *Concilia Galliae*, SL 148, ed. Charles Munier, (Brepols: Turnhout, 1963), 153.

[14] Bishop of Tours, b. 538(?), d. 594(?).

mulated his rule. In Gregory's accounts, we can at least sense some of the excesses and problems with which Grimlaicus had to deal.

There is Leobard, who took up residence in a solitary cell in the monastery of Saint Majorus near Tours. As his work, he prepares vellum for writing. He memorizes the Psalms, the better to understand the Scriptures. Leobard's conduct in his cell epitomizes the solitary's ideal: "He delighted in fasts, in prayer, in saying the Psalms, and in reading. He never stopped praying the divine offices and private prayer. Sometimes he wrote, to keep himself from indulging in harmful thoughts." [15] Because of a conflict that had arisen in the monastery, Leobard had thought of moving on, but Gregory himself remonstrated with him and, in order to teach him how an enclosed monk should behave, loaned him "books and the lives of the fathers and the institute of monks." [16] Leobard was much sought after as a guide for laypeople and rulers, and he constantly prayed for ecclesiastics. He cut his hair and beard at set times and did not pride himself on the length of his hair or beard. Many miracles of healing were performed through him. He had an attendant who looked after his needs. [17]

All of the features of Leobard's life are later dealt with in Grimlaicus' rule. Constant prayer, holy reading, manual work, stability, giving counsel—these are the staples of any monastic life, whether communal or solitary. But even the seemingly less central elements are of concern to Grimlaicus. He makes sure that solitaries shave and cut their hair fairly often, and he stipulates how the enclosed person is to act toward the disciple who acts as attendant and toward people who come seeking advice. [18] He is extremely wary of those who perform cures. [19]

---

[15] Gregory of Tours, *Vitae patrum*, 20; PL 71:1092–93.

[16] Ibid., 1094. *Librosque ei et vitas patrum ac institutionem monachorum.* The first item may refer to some part of the collections that have come down to us as *Vitae patrum.* The second may refer to Cassian's work, *De institutis coenobiorum.*

[17] Ibid., 1095.

[18] Chaps. 16 and 52–53.

[19] See chap. 67 and the story of Senoch, below.

Not all the stories Gregory relates are as edifying as that of Leobard, and most are not about solitaries in a cenobitic environment. Nonetheless, many of the accounts present a foil against which we can appreciate the stipulations that Grimlaicus puts into his rule. Anatolius, a twelve-year-old, persuaded his master to let him be enclosed. In the corner of an ancient crypt, there was a "little cell fashioned out of squared stones, in which one person, standing upright, could hardly fit." The boy stayed there for more than eight years, finally going mad. He pushed out through the wall of cut stones, screaming that he was being burned by God's saints. People took him to Tours where, by the help of Saint Martin, he seems to have been cured. But Anatolius went back to his cell and slipped back into madness.[20] One is reminded of Grimlaicus insistence that only a person who has been proven in cenobitic life and by prudent guides is to be allowed to enter a cell of reclusion.

Some solitaries thought up bizarre ascetical practices for themselves. Lupicinus lived in a cell near a village and used to sing psalms day and night. He kept himself awake during the day by tying a large stone around his neck. At night, he fixed two thorns to the top of the staff he leaned on, so that they would prick his chin if he dozed off. Eventually Lupicinus ruins his health and dies spitting up blood.[21] It is against the background of just such excesses that Grimlaicus stipulates a healthy daily regimen for solitaries. They are to get fresh air, decent food, and adequate clothing and bedding. For him, sickness or exceptional behavior are not signs of sanctity.

Grimlaicus' insistence that reclusion is a permanent commitment[22] can be set against the story of Senoch, a cleric who founded a monastery for himself, eventually being joined by three others. He closed himself up in a cell, chained by hands, feet, and neck.[23]

---

[20] Gregory of Tours, *Historia Francorum*, 8.34; PL 71:474.

[21] Gregory of Tours, *Vitae patrum*, 13; PL 71:1064–65.

[22] See, e.g., chap. 69.

[23] Gregory of Tours, *Vitae patrum*, 15; PL 71:1071–72. See Benedict's words, related in Grimlaicus' chapter 48, that the chain holding the enclosed person is love for Christ.

With donations given him, Senoch helped the poor, buying more than two hundred people out of slavery. Senoch left his cell to speak with Gregory. Eventually he became proud of his holiness and began visiting his relatives. Gregory scolds him, and Senoch is duly chastened. Since he cured people and yet also wanted to live the enclosed life, Gregory advises him to stay in his cell from the feast of Saint Martin, November 11, until Christmas and also during Lent. At other times he should go about and heal people. Gregory has an illuminating comment about performing signs to which Grimlaicus would subscribe: "He practiced rigorous abstinence and cured of their diseases those who were sick. But, just as holiness starts to encroach upon abstinence, so vanity starts to encroach upon holiness." [24]

Occasionally we read of monks who ruled their monasteries from reclusion. Salvius, after living many years under a rule in a monastery, became its abbot. After some time he concluded that it would be better to be "hidden among the monks than to be called abbot among the people." He bid the brothers farewell and had himself enclosed. He ministered to whomever sought him out and was generous with prayers and healing. [25] In the light of what Grimlaicus has to say about solitaries assuming ecclesial office, it is interesting to note that, after many years, Salvius was drawn out of his cell and made a bishop against his will. [26]

One final account from the works of Gregory is included here because nearly every element of the narrative occurs, more than three hundred years later, in the procedure detailed in the rule of Grimlaicus for receiving into reclusion. A young girl in the monastery of the abbess Radegund asks permission to be enclosed

[24] Ibid., 1072. See Grimlaicus' cautions about performing cures and other signs, in chaps. 67–68.

[25] Gregory of Tours, *Historia Francorum*, 7.1; PL 71:415.

[26] Ibid., 418. See Grimlaicus' chap. 22. Although not in Gregory's works, the account of Leonianus is instructive. For more than forty years, in the environs of Vienna and Augsburg, he was seen by no one, yet he took on responsibility not only for a community of monks but also a large monastery of nuns. "*Vita patrum Iurensium Romani, Lupicini, Eugendi*," in *Passiones vitaeque sanctorum aevi merovingici*, ed. Bruno Krusch, MGH *Scriptorum rerum Merovingicarum*, (Hannover: Hahn, 1896; repr. 1977), vol. 3, 156.

in a cell. Radegund questions her and determines that the girl in fact freely chooses to be enclosed. All the nuns gather, singing psalms and carrying lit candles. Radegund, holding the girl's hand, leads her to the cell. The girl kisses each of her sisters and bids them farewell. She is then enclosed, the door of the cell then being blocked. The new solitary then gives herself to prayer and reading.[27]

Sources and Style

This volume is a translation of Grimlaicus rule, not a study of its sources. We can note, however, some features of the way Grimlaicus used patristic and monastic authorities. In the prologue to his rule, Grimlaicus says that his work has consisted of collecting and collating.[28] His own words amount to next to nothing.[29] So that no one may confuse author and collator, Grimlaicus has noted the sources from which he excerpted the many examples and sayings he borrowed, sometimes mentioning the author in his text, sometimes putting the name in the margin. Unfortunately, copyists were not careful to obey Grimlaicus' injunction not to omit the names of his sources; the marginal notes were not passed down, and some names dropped out of the text.

Grimlaicus is not being falsely humble in calling himself a collector. In most chapters of his rule, he is careful to base his discussion of virtues and vices, regulations and conditions, upon accepted patristic and monastic authorities. The number and range of patristic and monastic sources that Grimlaicus used is impressive. He refers to a dozen patristic and monastic writers by name.[30] With regard to both number and length of citation, the Rule of Saint Benedict and the *Lives of the Fathers of the Desert* (the *Vitae patrum*,

---

[27] Gregory of Tours, *Historia Francorum*, 6.29; PL 71:396. See chap. 15 of Grimlaicus' rule.

[28] *decerpi . . . componere . . . compilatorem.*

[29] *mea dicta licet sint exigua*

[30] See Index of Patristic and Monastic Authors.

chiefly book 5), are far and away the most heavily used sources.[31] Julianus Pomerius, under the name Prosper of Aquitaine, and Jerome, especially his letters, form a kind of second tier. Other authors prominent in the list are Basil (by way of the *Codex regularum* and the *Concordia regularum*), Cassian, Gregory the Great (especially his homilies on the Gospels), and Isidore of Seville. When he cites ancient sources, Grimlaicus nearly always has a wording different from that found in modern editions. He probably retrieved a good number of his quotations, not from copies of the original works but from collections of sayings, anthologies of passages gleaned by monks from their reading and arranged under thematic headings. Grimlaicus uses the collection of sayings composed by Defensor of Ligugé known as *Liber scintillarum*, that is, *The Book of Sparks,* some thirteen times.[32] Indeed, sayings that occur together in Defensor sometimes occur together in Grimlaicus. As often as not, however, Grimlaicus' wording corresponds more closely to the original than to that found in Defensor's compilation. It looks as though Grimlaicus retrieved some of his citations of patristic and monastic authors from the collection made by Defensor (or one very much like it), but it also seems as though he sometimes went from the collection to the sources themselves.

In its extant form, the *Liber scintillarum* contains citations used by Grimlaicus from Jerome, Augustine, Caesarius (attributed to Augustine), Gregory the Great, Isidore, and the *Vitae patrum*. Similarly, Sedulius Scotus' *Collectaneum miscellaneum* has two citations from Jerome, only one of which is today verifiable as being Jerome's. When a quotation from a patristic source also occurs in these later collections, it is attributed in the Index of Patristic and Monastic Sources both to the original author and to the collector. In those

---

[31] Several of the apophthegms or stories from the *Vitae patrum* occur in multiple versions; citations given in the index point to that version to which Grimlaicus' version most closely corresponds.

[32] The *Liber scintillarum* was probably composed by Defensor, a monk of the abbey of Saint Martin at Ligugé, around 700. This compilation became extremely popular and is represented by 361 extant manuscripts. See the introduction to *Defensoris Locogiacensis monachi liber scintillarum*, ed. D. Henricus Rochais, OSB, CC, vol. 117 (Brepols, Turnhout, 1957).

few cases in which the collector attributes a saying to a patristic author but that saying cannot be located in the author's extant works, then it is listed only under the collector. Further research is needed to clarify precisely how Grimlaicus relied on collections made by Defensor and others and in what form he had direct or mediated access to ancient and early medieval sources.[33]

Here is a short example of the way Grimlaicus handles a source text. Generally, he adds phrases that apply the saying to the life of the enclosed contemplative or that explain the sometimes terse phrases of the original. He omits words that seem redundant or details that are beside the point he is making. In chapter 14 of the rule, he relates one of the apophthegms of the Desert Fathers. The text in italic is the saying as found in PL 73:858; the line beneath it is Grimlaicus' version.

> *Dixit iterum: Qui sedet in solitudine et quiescit*
> Qui enim in solitudine, hoc est in retrusione,
>
> *a tribus bellis eripitur, id est auditus, locutionis, et visus,*
> a tribus bellis eripitur, id est auditus, locutionis, et visus,
>
> *et contra unum tantummodo habebit pugnam*
> et contra unum tantummodo habebit pugnam
>
> *id est, cordis.*
> id est, cogitationem cordis.[34]

One of Grimlaicus' sources merits special mention: the Rule of Benedict. Grimlaicus is so completely conversant with the spirit and letter of Benedict's Rule that he seldom names it, even though he makes explicit use of it in half the chapters of his own rule.[35] As

---

[33] Curiously, Grimlaicus uses Defensor's collection only from chap. 37 on.

[34] Yet another version of this apophthegm is preserved in PG 65:78, 11: *Huiusmodi etiam oratio eius exstitit: Qui sedet in solitudine et quiescit a tribus bellis eripitur: auditus, locutionis, et visus; unum solum pugnare habet, nempe fornicationis.*

[35] Grimlaicus states in only three places that he is quoting from RB (in chaps. 53, 55, and 61). He refers to the figure of Benedict five further times (chaps. 43, 45, 48, 49, and 57). It is remarkable that these references all occur in the last third of the rule.

can be seen from the notes accompanying the translation, the framework of Benedict's Rule for monastic communities becomes the framework of Grimlaicus' rule for enclosed solitaries. Whether through quotation, adaptation, or allusion, the Rule of Benedict is discernible throughout all of Grimlaicus' text. As he does when citing patristic authors, Grimlaicus almost always alters the wording of Benedict's Rule to suit his purpose. Let this example from RB 1.4-5 and chapter 1 of the rule of Grimlaicus serve for many. The text in italic is from the former; the line beneath it is Grimlaicus' adaptation:

sed monasterii probatione diuturna, qui didicerunt
qui iam didicerant per multa experimenta

contra diabolum multorum solacio iam docti pugnare
contra diabolum pugnare,

et bene exstructi [sicut aurum fornacis]
ipsi quoque bene instructi atque sicut aurum in fornace probati,

fraterna ex acie ad singularem pugnam eremi
fraterna ex acie ad singularem pugnam eremi

securi iam sine consolatione alterius
securi iam sine consolatione alterius

sola manu vel brachio contra vitia carnis vel cogitationum
sola manu vel brachio contra vitia carnis vel cogitationum

Deo auxiliante, pugnare sufficiunt.
Deo auxiliante, dimicaturi pergebant.

The reference to gold being tried in the furnace (see Prov 27:21) anticipates the description of the sarabaites in the first chapter of Benedict's Rule (RB 1.6). Since the Rule of Benedict is such a special case among the sources for Grimlaicus' rule, citations from it are given in a separate index.

A compiler should compile, not alter, his sources. Yet Grimlaicus goes beyond respect for originals to sound a commonplace of ancient and medieval Christian authors: Gospel truth cannot be subservient to the rules of rhetoric and grammar.[36] Parallels abound.[37]

An especially trenchant phrasing of this theme comes from the pen of Gregory of Tours, some three centuries before Grimlaicus. Gregory says that, because he has no training in rhetoric and grammar, people will accuse him of having the effrontery of wanting to be considered an author. His writings have no grace or wit. They are devoid of organization and even confuse the gender of nouns and the case demanded by prepositions. Gregory's detractors ask him: Can the sluggish ox wrestle? Can the lazy donkey fly? Can the black crow turn into a white dove? Can murky pitch become white milk? Gregory answers them with not a little irony that he is working for them. He has described events briefly and in a coarse and muddy style; they can then go on to expatiate upon those things in their brilliant, well-educated verse.[38]

While there is surely some posturing in such protestations about style and grammar, Grimlaicus, Otfrid, and Gregory all want to assure their readers that they intend to speak in a language that fits their subject matter. They want to be "non-ciceronian," direct and simple, as befits a Christian.[39] The prolix and clever language of pagan authors has no place in a retelling of the Gospel story, or in

---

[36] See Augustine's coming to terms with the language of the Bible in *Confessions*, 3:5ff. and book 7:21–22, and in *Enarratio in Ps 138. 20*: "It is better that grammarians reproach us than that the people not understand." And Jerome in his commentary on Ezechiel: "It is not our job to avoid blunders in discourse but to discuss the obscurity of Holy Scripture with whatever words we can." *In Hiezechielem* 12.40.5.

[37] About thirty years before Grimlaicus wrote his rule, the monk Otfrid von Weissenburg, composing a German paraphrase of the Gospels, explains in a Latin dedicatory preface that German usage compels him to violate the rules of Latin grammar. In any case, it is good works, not rhetorical skill that God wants from us ("*Ad Liutbertum*" in *Otfrids Evangelienbuch*, ed. Oskar Erdmann & Edward Schröder, 5th ed. with Ludwig Wolff, *Altdeutsche Textbibliothek* 49 [Tübingen: Niemeyer, 1965], 4–7).

[38] Gregory of Tours, *Liber de gloria confessorum*, Praefatio; PL 71:829.

[39] See Benedikt Vollmann, "*Gregor IV (Gregor von Tours)*" in *Reallexikon für Antike und Christentum*, ed. Theodor Klauser et al. (Stuttgart: Anton Hiersemann, 1981), 926–27.

narratives about Frankish saints, or in a rule for enclosed contemplatives. The Gospel and the Fathers are plain and easy to understand. To look there for fancy prose and flawless grammar is to miss the entrance to the kingdom, too low for the high and mighty yet open to the merest children.

Central Features of Grimlaicus' Teaching

Grimlaicus is careful to say what sort of solitaries he is legislating for: not anchorites, that is, hermits who dwell all by themselves, but cenobitic solitaries, that is, those who dwell in the midst of a *cenobium* but who live in quarters sealed off from most physical contact with others. The cell's situation within the monastic enclosure and the solitary's remaining under the authority of rule and abbot eliminate many of the excesses practiced by solitaries who lived without the guidance and discipline provided by a monastic community. The daily round of Divine Office, Mass, *lectio divina*, meals, work, spiritual conferences, and so on, supports a life both spiritually and physically healthy.

It is not the purpose of this introduction to describe in detail the life and surroundings of cenobitic solitaries or to trace the history of this style of monastic living before and after Grimlaicus. That has been done by others.[40] It is simply noted here that the sort of life for which Grimlaicus legislated was by no means rare. From the middle of the sixth century, many European monasteries had solitaries living in cells, whether within the monastic enclosure or attached to the church. The most frequently attested case is that of males enclosed in monasteries of monks. Nevertheless, female solitaries sometimes lived attached to monasteries both of monks and of nuns, and, very rarely, male solitaries lived attached to monasteries of women.[41]

---

[40] For a description of the life of enclosed solitaries in southern Germany during the early Middle Ages, see Otmar Doerr, *Das Institut der Inclusen in Süddeutschland, Beiträge zur Geschichte des alten Mönchtums und des Benedictinerordens* 18 (Münster: Aschendorff, 1934), especially 32–56.

[41] Gougaud, 77–82. See also Doerr, 32, and the introduction by Brockie, who says that cells of recluses were still to be seen in many ancient monasteries, 292.

There is no need to summarize Grimlaicus' teaching. His own words are the best guide for understanding his ideal of the life of a cenobitic *retrusus*. It may be helpful, however, to highlight those elements that demonstrate Grimlaicus' good sense and Benedictine fondness for moderation. Some elements have already been touched on in the consideration of the solitaries who people the works of Gregory of Tours. One who aspires to the life of reclusion is to undergo a lengthy period of testing. Due attention is to be paid to hygiene and health, both of one's person and one's surroundings. Beyond such particulars, however, Grimlaicus centers the life of the solitary squarely within the life of the larger community and of the church, a life that entails very concrete and very serious responsibilities. If an enclosed solitary is called to assume gover-nance and has the requisite talent, then, Grimlaicus unhesitatingly says, that person must accept the burden of leadership. The reasons for his judgment are entirely ecclesial: gifts are for the benefit of all, not just of oneself; the Son came forth from the Father for the good of us all; the test of love is service; the humility that refuses to assume the responsibilities of leadership is false.[42]

Solitaries in cells of retrusion serve the whole body of the church, not only by prayer, but also by giving sound counsel and, in the case of priests, hearing confessions. They dispense a wide variety of teaching to a wide range of the faithful. No one is for-mally committed to their care, hence solitaries teach and exhort solely through love for those who come to them.[43]

Beyond any authority they may be asked to assume, beyond any particular advice they may give, solitaries are to build up the church by giving good example to everyone and, most immediately and importantly, by encouraging and supporting those few people with whom they have contact: the one or two other solitaries who are there with them, and their disciple(s).[44]

If we were to ask which part of the rule seems to be Grimlaicus' particular teaching, which section offers the clearest insight into

[42] Chap. 22.
[43] Chap. 20.
[44] Chaps. 21, 52–53, and 62.

his unique view of the enclosed life and even into his personality, the answer would be chapters 8–28. In these chapters Grimlaicus relies far less on citations from acknowledged authorities than elsewhere in his rule.[45]

Although Grimlaicus speaks in his own words in these chapters, he says nothing that cannot be found in the monastic and contemplative tradition. In particular, the knowledge of human nature, moderation, and concern for the wider community testify to the wholesome influence of the Rule of Benedict. On every page of Grimlaicus' rule, and especially in these chapters, we sense that, like his master, Saint Benedict, Grimlaicus has compassion for human frailty but knows to what heights that person can ascend who aims at the substance of virtue rather than at its trappings and who prefers nothing to the love of Christ.

Chapters 27 and 28, two of the longest chapters in the rule, are unique. Here Grimlaicus is not compiling or legislating but exhorting, even lamenting. In his day, virtue has vanished, and everything is going to wrack and ruin. People who should be scaling the heights of virtue and contemplation are worried about their own comfort. He knows what he is talking about; he himself has been tepid in devotion and overly concerned about creature comforts. He hopes that his rule may encourage those who are living or intend to live the enclosed life (and here we may include those who want to learn from it or be inspired by it) to aim at nothing short of total self-donation.[46] Life in union with Christ in the Spirit in this life and everlasting life with God and the angels and saints in the next are the only goals worth pursuing. Grimlaicus urges all

---

[45] Chapters 8–13, 17, and 23–24 are almost completely without identifiable citations.

[46] Of the thirteen extant manuscripts of Grimlaicus' rule, six are included in codices along with patristic and early medieval material for *lectio divina*. It seems to have had appeal, not solely to solitaries, but to monks generally. See Marie-Christine Chartier, "*Reclus - En Occident*," in *Dictionnaire de spiritualité acétique et mystique*, ed. M. Viller et al., vol. 13, cols. 227–28 (Paris: Beauchesne, 1988). Grégoire (1043) indicates that several manuscripts were copied in cenobitic contexts, e.g., Saint-Remy at Rheims and the Cistercian abbey at Clairvaux.

his readers to get on with this holy work, to let nothing frighten them, and never to despair of God's mercy.

References to the Scriptures, RB, and Other Sources

In the translation, exact and nearly exact quotations from the Vulgate are given between quotation marks, with the citation following immediately in brackets. Such references are compiled in the Index of Scriptural References. In cases where Grimlaicus paraphrases a Scripture passage or conflates it with a similar one, the text will not be put between quotation marks, and the reference in brackets will be preceded by "See." The English rendering from the Vulgate is that of the translator.

When the beginning and end of a nonscriptural citation can be established, the whole is given between quotation marks. The reader should keep in mind, however, that, when Grimlaicus refers to nonscriptural sources, he nearly always alters them to a greater or lesser extent. All such references are listed in the Index of Patristic and Monastic Authors.

The Rule of Benedict permeates the rule of Grimlaicus. He seldom quotes the text of RB exactly, having worked Benedict's words into his own. Therefore, to set off citatations of RB with quotation marks would not only overburden the page with punctuation but also mislead the reader. Rather, in all cases reference is made in footnotes to the pertinent section of RB. The Index of Citations from the Rule of Saint Benedict compiles all of these footnoted references.

Note on Terminology

The rule of Grimlaicus is a Carolingian document. It looks to the Rule of Benedict and to patristic and early monastic authorities for its teaching and vocabulary. Distinctions and subtleties of the Cistercians and the scholastics lie in the future. Several terms, however, demand particular attention: *conversatio, animus,* and *anima.*

Two senses of *conversatio* can be distinguished: (1) turning or conversion to monastic life and (2) the monastic way of life itself as demanding constant conversion. Modern translations of the Rule of Benedict (McCann, *RB 1980*, and Kardong) render *conversatio* by a wide range of terms, depending on the context: monastic life, conversion, way of life, lifestyle, observance, holy life, date of conversion, being a monk, date of entry, monastic observance.[47] In Grimlaicus' rule, *conversatio* most often has the general meaning "way of life," "mode of acting." It sometimes has, however, a more specialized meaning, that of an ascetic way of life or monastic observance. The term is noted each time it occurs.[48]

Animus has an extremely wide spectrum of meanings in patristic and early monastic writings. The term's center of gravity, so to speak, is in thinking and willing; it often corresponds to the English terms understanding, will, mind, intention, and resolve. Yet *animus* is often used to speak of what we call the heart, feelings, temper, or, more generally, spirit. The word can be used to speak of the self, one's person, one's true self. Set phrases with *animus* are frequent: *ex animo*, "from the heart"; *duplex animo*, "of two minds"; *bono animo*, "cheerfully"; *malo animo*, "with bad will." Grimlaicus' text reflects this general situation. It would be misleading to render every occurrence of *animus* by the same English word. Context must determine the proper equivalent: what terms is *animus* coordinated with or opposed to; of what verb is it the subject or object; does it refer to the whole person or to a specific faculty of the person? Because *animus* is patient of such a wide range of meanings, every occurrence of the word in this translation will be noted.

Anima occurs most often in early monastic works in quotations from the Psalms in Latin, where it means one's life, one's self. In addition, *anima* is the word Christian authors use to speak about the soul as separated from the body after death. It also occurs with the sense of heart, affections. This translation renders *anima* as "soul."

[47] *The Rule of Saint Benedict in Latin and English*, ed. and trans. Justin McCann (Westminster, MD: Newman, 1952); *RB 1980: The Rule of Saint Benedict in Latin and English with Notes*, ed. Timothy Fry et al. (Collegeville, MN: Liturgical Press, 1981); Terrence Kardong, *Benedict's Rule: A Translation and Commentary* (Collegeville, MN: Liturgical Press, 1996).

[48] The results of scholarship concerning the term *conversatio* are summarized in *RB 1980*, 459–63.

Some of the rule's chapters or parts thereof speak specifically about a single *inclusus* (for example, 15). Others address the situation of solitaries who are priests (for example, 18). Still others refer exclusively to males (for example, 37). Apart from such instances, this translation makes use of plural nouns and plural, indefinite, and second-person pronouns in English when the Latin text employs the masculine singular. Grimlaicus himself gives warrant for such renderings, since he shifts easily and frequently between the singular and plural of nouns and uses various indefinite, masculine singular, and first-person-plural pronouns in close proximity.

Chapter Headings

Chapter 24: On the Same Topic as the Previous Chapter

Chapter 25: The Tools of Good Works

Chapter 26: Observing God's Commandments

Chapter 27: A Deplorable Description of Those Who Do Not
Observe Christ's Precepts

Chapter 28: Continuing the Same Lamentation as Above

Chapter 29: Compunction of Heart

Chapter 30: The Two Kinds of Compunction

Chapter 31: Concerning Reverence and Persistence in Prayer

Chapter 32: How Someone Can Pray Without Ceasing

Chapter 33: All Empty Thoughts Are Illusions Worked by
Demons

Chapter 34: God and the Angels Are Always Present to Those
Who Are Singing and Chanting Psalms

Chapter 35: The Praise of the Psalms and the Arrangement of
the Hours at Which We Ought to Sing Psalms

Chapter 36: Whether Anyone Should Dare to Receive the Body
of the Lord or to Chant Mass Every Day

Chapter 37: Whether Someone May Celebrate Mass or Not, after
the Illusion That Sometimes Happens in Dreams

Chapter 38: Constancy in Reading and Prayer

Chapter 39: The Daily Manual Work of Solitaries

Chapter 40: At Certain Hours Solitaries Should Be Occupied in
Manual Labor

Chapter 41: Solitaries Should Have Nothing of Their Own and
Should Accept the Offerings of the Faithful

Chapter 42: The Hours at Which Solitaries Ought to Take
Their Meals

The Rule for Solitaries

In the Name of the Most High God
Begins the Prologue of the Rule for Solitaries

To my most dear father in Christ, who has the same name as I do, to Grimlaicus, the venerable priest, everlasting salvation in the Savior.

Whenever I disclosed to you privately what displeased me about myself, you would very often suggest that I should put in writing a rule for solitaries, that is, cenobitic solitaries, and place upon myself a yoke of service.[1] For a long time I did all I could to refrain from doing this, since I was afraid that it might exceed my powers and, more importantly, that I might run and fall headlong into the sin of pride. I feared both that some people might think I was so presumptuous as to found something new and that the ancient proverb might be thrown at me: What's the use of throwing a fish in the sea or water in a river? But after many days I began to recall that it was not the custom of our holy forebears to provoke or to envy one another; rather each of them contributed what each one

---

[1] "Yoke" (*iugum*) and "service, servitude" (*servitus*) are often used to refer to the monastic way of life and the obligations it entails (see RB 58.16; 49.5; and 50.4).

could to set God's house in order. And so I chose to comply with your command rather than to do my own will. Consequently I soon set myself to work at the task assigned me. To this end I excerpted various sayings and examples of the orthodox fathers and have contented myself with fashioning this rule from them. In order to keep the chapters from being too lengthy, I have inscribed the names of those whose sayings I included in this work sometimes in the text and sometimes outside in the margins. I have been very careful to do this to keep people from naming the compiler as the author. For I know, as the Lord said, that "those who speak on their own are seeking their own glory" [John 7:18]. Even though my own words are very trifling, nonetheless I have been careful to mark them by my own usual name in among the flowers of the sayings of the saints. For this reason, I humbly beg whoever thinks this rule worth copying not to neglect to note the aforesaid names of the saints, just as they are here noted.[2] I have not worried about keeping in this little work barbarisms and turns of speech that reflect our language and the cases they use after prepositions, since I believe I would be most culpable if I were to constrain the words of Christ or of the holy fathers by the rules of Donatus.[3]

What I have done, then, is to excerpt this rule from the flowers of the saints, as though from river channels and from ocean depths, and divided them into little streams, that is, into sixty-nine chapters. First of all I have collected a few chapters about renouncing the world and about the active and contemplative lives. Next how the solitary way of life should be established,[4] followed by some chapters about the life and conduct of solitaries. Among these I have inserted only three chapters about the precepts of our Redeemer,

---

[2] The identification of sources that Grimlaicus asks for has not come down to us.

[3] Grimlaicus' disclaimer about his uncouth style mirrors that of Gregory the Great at the end of the dedicatory letter to his *Moralia in Hiob*, PL 75:516.

[4] *solitaris conversatio constare*. The term *conversatio* is roughly equivalent to "monastic way of living." It is used ten times in the Rule of Benedict. See the introduction and also the discussion in *RB 1980*, 459, and the concordance entry on 506.

to the end that solitaries may meditate day and night on the law of the Lord [see Ps 1:2] and may turn the commandments of Christ over and over again before the eyes of both mind and body and so become more devout and fervent. Thereafter I come to the active life and have laid down what and how much food and drink, what clothing and bedding they are to have or use. I have also included the manner and time of fasting and abstaining. I have also added at suitable spots a few words about the virtues and vices, and, in order to put solitaries on their guard, I have taken care to indicate how they should act in working miracles. Finally I have set down a single chapter about persevering in this good work.

Throughout these chapters, therefore, wherever it was necessary to explain some clauses, I have tried to imitate the way a river acts. As a river is flowing along in its bed, if it happens upon sunken valleys off to the side, it immediately diverts its flow into them; when it has filled them up, it promptly flows back into its bed. In the same way, whenever I have found among the sacred words of the saints some obscure passage that promised to yield suitable instruction, I turned my current, as it were, into the nearby valley of explanation. Once I had sufficiently explored that valley of obscurity, I ran back again to the riverbed of my main theme. I proceeded in this way, not because it was my own idea or desire, but because the sayings of the holy fathers approved of it.

I call as witnesses both you, venerable father, who have prompted me to complete this little work, as well as all those who perhaps may read it, and I beg you: if you find anything objectionable among the matters that are set out here, then please blame it on my boorishness and be so kind as to pardon me. But those words you approve of as being according to the Catholic faith, ascribe them "to God who gives to everyone abundantly and does not reproach" [James 1:5]. But I who am trying to fulfill the precept of the one who orders it[5] have presumed to take on things that are too much for me. But was it not absolutely imperative that I obey? This opportunity has provided me with a rule that I did not have

---

[5] I.e., who told him to write down the rule.

before and now have. Besides, I have not bothered with the niceties
of educated diction, since I cannot display in speaking what I was
not able to learn from my teachers.

However, I finished what I wrote, relying not on my own talent
but on the help of your prayers. To heal someone who asks them,
physicians prepare a medicinal compound out of many different
types of herbal preparations, and they are not so presumptuous as
to claim that they created the herbs or the other kinds of plants.
No, they admit that they are merely assistants who collect and
prepare them. That is what I am: I am not the author of this work
but just the assistant who collected it. From the compound made
up of these different kinds of plants, sick people will be healed. In
this way then, perhaps the labor to which I have devoted myself
will be able, with God's help, to be of some profit to your charity.
I assume that you would not have directed me so insistently to
write down this rule unless you loved it and unless you yourself
desired at some time to undertake the solitary life. Just as you have
shown me the affection of loving devotion and exhorted me to
write down this rule, so now I humbly plead with you to devote
yourself to reading it carefully and often, so that your soul may, so
to speak, become weary of exterior troubles, return to itself, and
realize where it should hurry to. What is more tiring in this life
than to be on fire with earthly desires? Or what is safer than to
crave nothing of this world's vanity? Those who love this world
are distressed by its troublesome cares and worries. But those who
withdraw from the world and seek out the solitary life begin to
have to some extent in this life the peaceful rest that they hope to
have in the life to come.

Consequently I ask both you and all those who love God neither to spurn this rule nor to be terrified and flee from this instruction, because the path of salvation can be begun in no other way
than by a narrow beginning. As the Lord says: "Strive to enter
through the narrow gate" [Luke 13:24], and also: Cramped and
narrow is the path that leads to life; broad and spacious the one that
leads to death [see Matt 7:13-14]. In what I have drawn up I hope
to have written nothing harsh or burdensome, nothing onerous.
But if, following the dictates of sound reason, I have stipulated

anything that is somewhat strict, I have done this to correct vices and preserve virtues.[6]

Therefore, if you want to observe this rule with a good spirit and complete devotion, even while you are still in this present world, you can, with God's help, climb to the peak of virtue. And when this life has ended, you can reign with the holy and chosen ones of God in the heavenly kingdom and live happily forever with the Lord himself and his angels, and not only live but even reign with him. May almighty God quickly lead you[7] to observe what has been set down here, and by your observing it, may God lead you to heavenly kingdoms. Amen.

Here begins the text of the Rule.

Chapter 1: The Kinds of Solitaries

We must first indicate why someone is called a "monk" or "solitary," and then, with God's gracious help, proceed to explain other matters. The word monk [*monachus*] comes from Greek and means that a person is single [*singularis*]. *Monas* is Greek for the Latin singleness [*singularitas*]. Hence "solitary" gives the meaning of the word "monk." That is why, whether one says "monk" or "solitary," it is one and the same thing.

But let us see how many kinds of solitaries there are. There are two kinds of solitaries: one is anachorites, that is, hermits; the other is cenobites, that is, those who live in monasteries. Neither of these kinds should be instituted in the first fervor of conversion, but they should first be given a prolonged testing in the observance of the monastery,[8] so that, once they have been tested, they may have the strength to rise, by the Lord's mercy, up to the summit of perfection.

---

[6] The foregoing lines follow closely RB Prol. 46–48.
[7] *animum vestrum*
[8] See RB 1.3.

Further, "many people have wondered who was the very first monk who began to live in the desert. Some people go back very far and say that it began with the blessed Elijah and John [the Baptist]. Others maintain that blessed Anthony was the first to conceive this intention. But Macarius, the disciple of blessed Anthony, attests that," in New Testament times, "a certain Paul of Thebes was the first person to adopt this mode of life."⁹ And that is true. It should be known, however, that it was from the time of blessed Anthony that there began to be cenobitic solitaries, that is, recluses. But it is difficult to ascertain who was the first recluse, since recluses used to live not only in cenobia but also in the very desert itself. In fact, in ancient times, those who had first been recluses in monasteries and who had learned through many trials to fight against the devil and who had been well taught and tested like gold in the furnace, would go out from the battle line of their brothers to single combat; safe now without the support of another, with only their hand or arm, they would go out to struggle, with God's help, against the vices of the flesh or the thoughts.¹⁰

The blessed bishop Arnulf¹¹ followed the example of these monks. According to the Lord's precept, he sold all he had and distributed it to the poor. And he not only left behind all his earthly possessions, but he even gave up the episcopacy which the Lord had bestowed on him and which he had taken up after he had lost every temporal possession. Thereafter he sought out a cell in which to be a recluse.¹² There for many days he surrendered himself to the Lord to exert himself in the worship of God. Finally, after many years had run their course, he took on wings like a dove, that is, spiritual virtues, and flew away to the desert [see Ps 54:7]. There he hoped in our Lord Jesus Christ, that he would save him from

---

⁹ Jerome, *Vita sancti Pauli primi eremitae*, Prologue; PL 23:17–18.

¹⁰ See RB 1.4-6.

¹¹ Bishop of Metz, died 640. A life of him attributed to Paul the Deacon is found in PL 95:731–40, and a version edited by Krusch in MGH, *Scriptores rerum Merovingicarum: Fredegarii et aliorum chronica. Vita sanctorum*, 426ff.

¹² *cellula retrusionis*

timidity of spirit and from the tempest. The Lord came and not only saved him but transported him to the heavens to crown him.

I wanted to include here the example of such a great man, so that solitaries might learn from him to despise all perishable things and to long for heavenly things with all their strength.

Chapter 2: The Loftier Precepts Concerning Monks or Solitaries

The precepts that are given to monks and to those who renounce this world are loftier than those given to the faithful who are leading an ordinary life in the world. To monks and solitaries it is said: "If you wish to be perfect, go and sell all you have and give to the poor and come, follow me" [Matt 19:21], and also: "Everyone who leaves home or brothers and sisters or father or mother or wife or children or fields on account of my name will receive a hundredfold and will possess eternal life" [Matt 19:29]. These and similar precepts apply especially to monks living alone and to solitaries. And the more exceptional the precepts are, the more powerful and preeminent they are. But the words that follow are, as it were, lesser precepts spoken in general to everyone: The Lord says: "Those who do not take up their cross and come after me are not worthy of me" [Matt 10:38]. And also: "Everything that you want people to do to you, do that to them" [Matt 7:12]; "but I say to you: Do not resist an evil person" [Matt 5:39]. He also says: "Love your enemies; do good to those who hate you" [Matt 5:44], and so on.

Monks and solitaries are told to abandon all that is theirs; people in the world are told to use well what is theirs. The former, by living well, transcend the general precepts; the latter are bound to the general precepts. In order to reach perfection, it is not enough to abandon what one has, unless one also denies oneself. But what does "to deny oneself" mean, except to renounce one's own acts of will?[13] In this way, whoever was proud may become humble;

---

[13] See RB Prol. 3.

whoever was prone to anger may become forbearing; whoever was dissolute may become chaste; whoever before was drunken may become sober; whoever was envious and spiteful may become kind and considerate. For if you renounce everything that you have yet do not renounce your own way of acting, you are certainly not Christ's disciple. If you renounce your possessions, you are renouncing what belongs to you, but if you renounce your wicked way of acting, you are renouncing yourself. That is why the Lord says: "Those who want to come after me, let them deny themselves and follow me" [Luke 9:23].

Chapter 3: The Four Orders of People That Will Be on the Day of Judgment

You should also know that, on the day of judgment, there will be four orders of people, two of good people and two of bad. The first order will be saved and not judged, that is, those who leave all that they have for the sake of Christ. These people will come to the judgment as judges with God. This is what Isaiah is speaking about: "The Lord will come to judgment with the elders of his people" [Isa 3:14]. These people will judge others and will not be judged by others.

The second order will be judged and will be saved, that is, good Christians who possess things of this world and who dispense them every day to the poor, who clothe the naked, visit the sick, and fulfill duties like these that Christ teaches us to do [see Matt 25:31–46]. These people will be judged and will be saved. To them the Lord will say at the judgment: "I was hungry and you fed me" [Matt 25:35], and a little further:[14] "Come, blessed of my Father; take possession of the kingdom that has been prepared for you from the beginning of the world" [Matt 25:34].

The third order will likewise be judged and will be condemned, that is, bad Christians, who seem to have faith but who do not put it into action. These people will be destined for the left side at the

---

[14] Actually these words come in the previous verse.

judgment, and to them the Lord himself will say: "I was hungry and you did not feed me; I was thirsty and you did not give me something to drink" [Matt 25:42], and a little further:[15] "Go, you cursed, into the eternal fire that has been prepared for the devil and his angels" [Matt 25:41]. These people will be judged and will not be saved.

The fourth order will be that of unbelievers, who will not be judged and will not be saved but will be condemned. About these people the psalmist says: "The wicked will not rise up at the judgment, nor sinners in the council of the just" [Ps 1:5]. The wicked will indeed rise, not to be judged but to be condemned, that is to say, those "who sinned without the Law will perish without the Law" [Rom 2:12].

But the first order, the people who left what they had and followed Christ, will judge the two next orders, that is, they will see that good Christians receive good things, and conversely, that bad Christians receive bad things. With the most fervent devotion, then, let us beg God to touch our hearts with his mercy and make us despise all visible things, that we may be able to belong to the first order. By living our lives well, let us lay claim to this great grace: that if we guard our life perfectly, we will be judges at the judgment with God and his apostles. We ought to believe this most firmly, because the One who promised it to us is most faithful. He himself is truth; he cannot deceive. Solitaries who, for the love of Christ, leave all that they have, can say with the apostle Peter: "Lord, look, we have left everything and have followed you. What will be ours?" [Matt 19:27]. We should know for certain that the answer he gave to Peter he gives to all solitaries in Peter.

Perhaps someone will say: I want to imitate those who despise this world, but I don't have anything to leave. The answer to such an objection is: That person renounces a great deal who renounces the will to have. We should also note that he did not just say: "You who have left everything," but added "and have followed me" [Matt 19:28], because many people leave their possessions but do

---

[15] Again, these words occur in the previous verse.

not follow Christ. Such were Crates the philosopher and many others.[16] That person follows Christ who imitates him.

Peter spoke so confidently. Let us therefore think about what he renounced. All he left were nets and a boat, yet he says confidently: "We have left everything." It is as though he said: "Lord, we have done what you commanded. Now we want to know what sort of reward you will give us for doing that." But Jesus replies not only to them but to others: "Amen, I tell you that you who have followed me, in the rebirth, when the Son of Man will sit upon the throne of his majesty, you too will sit on twelve thrones and judge the twelve tribes of Israel" [Matt 19:28]. We have been promised great happiness and inexpressible glory. This pronouncement pertains to all who renounce everything they have for the love of God.

Let us rise above all visible things; let us despise all passing things, so that with the blessed apostles we may deserve to enjoy the glory of eternal blessedness. And so that this may happen quickly, let us humbly entreat the Lord's compassion every day and say: All-powerful God, who redeemed us through the blood of your Son and willed to give us new birth from water and the Holy Spirit, make us quickly pass from this most wretched pilgrimage to the native land we have so long desired, in which, with the blessed angels and those most happy people who renounced the world, we may reign for infinite ages.

Chapter 4: What True Riches Are

Blessed Gregory clearly indicates what true riches are when he says: "Only those riches are true which make us rich in the virtues."[17] Blessed Prosper shows clearly which riches we should crave and which we should flee from, when he says:

---

[16] Crates was a Cynic philosopher of the late fourth century BC. Jerome mentions Crates in connection with Peter's question and Christ's answer in his *Commentarium in evangelium Matthaei*, 3, on Matthew 19:27-28; PL 26:144.

[17] Gregory the Great, XL *Homiliae in evangelia*, 1.15.1; PL 76:1132.

We should seek to gain those riches which can both adorn and fortify us, arm us against enemy attacks, separate us from the world, commend us to God, and enrich and ennoble our souls. They ought to be with us and within us. We should believe that our riches are: modesty, which makes us modest; justice, which makes us just; devotion, which makes us devoted; humility, which makes us humble; forbearance, which makes us forbearing; innocence, which makes us innocent; purity, which makes us pure; prudence, which makes us prudent; temperance, which makes us temperate; and above all charity, which makes us dear to God and to human beings, powerless to commit sin, despising the world and pursuing every good. These are the virtues, not of everyone, but only of the saints. These are the property, not of the haughty rich, but of the humble poor. They are the inheritance of hearts, the incorruptible riches of one's conduct. The only people who have these virtues in abundance are they who renounce carnal things from the heart. Although carnal things are good, inasmuch as they were created by God, nevertheless since both good and bad people have them, spiritual people make it a point to despise them. They do this so that they may reach the incomparably better things that are the special possession of all good people. The good that bad people also have is not like the good that only good people have. When wicked people have a physical good, it is their reward; when just people have it, it is not their reward but a temporal comfort. In the same way, the loss of a temporal good becomes training for the just person and torture for the unjust. That is because the just are held fast by the desire for heaven; they do not sense whether they have or whether they lose all temporal goods. The wicked who take pleasure in having do not lose without sorrow. That is why those people who do battle for God[18] must flee riches with all their heart. Whoever wants to have riches does not seek them without labor, does not find them without difficulty, does not keep them without worry, does not possess them without anxious delight, and does not lose them without grievous sorrow. The Apostle, however, says to Christ's soldiers: "I want you to be without worry" [1 Cor 7:32], and also:

[18] See RB Prol. 3.

"The root of all evils is avarice. Some people, in craving for it, have strayed from the faith and brought themselves into many sorrows" [1 Tim 6:10]. And so, earthly property, for those who love it sinfully, is the cause not of pleasures but of sorrows.[19]

Let these words suffice concerning true and false wealth. Let us now hear how someone can ascend to the summit of perfection.

Chapter 5: The Perfection of Justice

If we want to be perfect, we should take up our cross and follow the Lord our Savior, and imitate Peter who said: "Lord, behold, we have left everything and have followed you" [Matt 19:27]. We should do what the Lord commanded the young man and what will suffice to make us perfect, that is: "Go and sell all you have and give to the poor, and come follow me" [Matt 19:21]. Both are in our power: to wish to be perfect and not to. The Lord does not force us by putting a yoke on us but allows us to use our free will, as he says: "Do you want to be perfect" and to stand at the pinnacle of dignity? "Sell all you have and give to the poor, and come follow me" [Matt 19:21]. If therefore you want to be perfect, sell all you have, and not just part of it, as did Ananias and Sapphira [see Acts 5:1-11]. No, sell all of it, and when you have sold it, do not pilfer anything but give the whole amount to the poor. That is how you will provide yourself with treasure for the kingdom of heaven.

But this alone does not make you perfect, unless, after having despised riches, you follow the Savior, leaving evil deeds behind and doing good ones. As Saint Jerome says, "It is easier to despise a moneybag than self-will and pleasure. Many people leave riches behind yet do not follow the Lord. That person is following the Lord who imitates him and goes forward in his footsteps. 'The

---

[19] Julianus Pomerius, *De vita contemplativa*, 2.13; PL 59:456–57. Seven times in his rule, Grimlaicus cites this work of Julianus Pomerius (died ca. 500), which was later attributed to Prosper of Aquitaine. It was held in high esteem and was widely popular throughout the Middle Ages.

person who says: I abide in Christ, should walk as Christ walked' [1 John 2:6]." [20]

Hence it is good for God's servant to be physically at a distance from the world, but it is much better to be so in will. To be both is the height of perfection. That person, therefore, is perfect who is separated from the world in both body and heart. That person will shine with great grace in the presence of God whom this world has held in contempt. Everything in this world should be inimical to God's servants, so that, as they perceive that these things are opposed to them, they should be on fire with a more ardent desire for heaven. What is more tiring in this life than to be on fire with earthly desires? Or what is safer than to crave nothing of this world's vanity? Those who love this world are distressed by its troublesome cares and worries. But those who withdraw from this world for the sake of that quiet which is inner peace begin to have to some extent in this life the peaceful rest that they hope to have in the life to come.

Chapter 6: Those Who Renounce the World Should Have Neither Inheritances Nor Possessions

Those who abandon the world completely ought to possess nothing except the Lord. That is why we read in the book of Prosper:

> If you are intent on possessing, then with eager mind possess God whom you worship and who possesses everything, and then you will have in God whatever you want with holy desire. But because you only possess God if you are possessed by God, first be God's possession. In this way God becomes both your possessor and your portion. What more do you then want, since your Creator has become everything for you? Or what is enough for you, for whom God himself is not enough? The one who spoke the words in the Spirit possessed God and was possessed by him: "O Lord, my portion, I have said that I will

---

[20] Jerome, *Commentarium in evangelium Matthaei*, 3.19; PL 26:142.

keep your law" [Ps 118:57], and also: "The Lord is the share
of my inheritance and of my cup" [Ps 15:5].[21]

If you possess the Lord and say with the prophet: "The Lord is
my portion" [Lam 3:24], you can have nothing besides the Lord.
If you were to have something besides the Lord, then the Lord
would not be your portion. If, for example, you had gold or silver
or possessions or various household goods, the Lord would not
consent to be your portion along with these portions. "If therefore," as Jerome says, "I am 'the Lord's portion and the cord of his
inheritance' [Deut 32:9], I will not accept a portion along with the
other tribes but, like a Levite and a priest, I will live from tithes;
I will serve the altar and will take my sustenance from the offerings
made on the altar. From there I will have food and clothing, and
with these I will be content, and, naked, I will follow the naked
cross."[22]

It was also said to Ezechiel: My priests, who minister to me in
my temple, shall not have possessions. Therefore the Lord will be
their possession. Neither shall they have an inheritance; I the Lord
am their inheritance [see Ezek 44:28]. And the Lord himself says
elsewhere to the sons of Levi: You shall not give a portion among
their brothers; I the Lord am their portion [see Num 18:20]. These
words suffice to make it clear that those who hold in contempt
the portion that is an earthly inheritance ought to show that they
are a people who possess the Lord and who are possessed by the
Lord.

On this same subject, an example is given in the conferences
of the fathers.

> A certain brother renounced the world and gave what he had
> to the poor, but he kept back a few things for his own use.
> This brother came to Abba Anthony. When the elder recog-
> nized him, he said: If you want to be a monk, go into that
> village over there and buy pieces of meat and put them on
> your naked body and come back here. And when he had done
> that, birds tore at the meat and at his body. When he had

[21] Julianus Pomerius, *De vita contemplativa*, 2.16; PL 59:460.
[22] Jerome, Ep 52.5; PL 22:531.

reached the elder, the latter asked him if he had done what he had ordered him. The brother showed him his lacerated body. Then holy Anthony said: Those who renounce the world and want to have riches will be attacked like this and will be torn to pieces by demons.[23]

This saying should be enough on the subject of not having possessions.

We will relate another saying about not having an inheritance. "A certain man named Magistratus came to the blessed Arsenius to bring him the testament of one of his close relatives who had left him a very large inheritance. When the elder took the testament, he wanted to tear it up. But Magistratus fell down at his feet and said: I beg you, for God's sake, do not tear it up. And Abba Arsenius said to him: I died before he did. He has just recently died, so how can he now make me his heir? He sent back the testament and did not take anything from it."[24] From this example we should understand that those who leave the world should have nothing except food and should possess nothing except clothing. In a special way, the solitary, who desires to imitate the apostles, ought to be content with only these things. A person cannot serve God and the world at the same time. That is why God wants those who worship him to renounce everything. Then, when they have gotten rid of desire for the world, God's love can grow and even become perfect in them.

Chapter 7: After Renouncing the World, a Person Should Not Save up Riches

Once solitaries have completely renounced the world, they should be so dead to the world that they delight in living for God alone. The more they withdraw from the desire to possess this world, the more they will contemplate with inner attention the

---

[23] *Vitae patrum*, 5.6.1; PL 73:888. Another version of this story is found in 6.68; PL 73:772.

[24] Ibid., 5.6.2; PL 73:888, where the man is named Magistrianus, not Magistratus. He begs the abba not to tear up the document, because, if it is destroyed, he will lose his head.

presence of God and of his saints. Many there are, however, who would flock to the grace of God but who are afraid of going without worldly pleasures. The love of Christ calls them forth but desire for the world calls them back. We read in the conferences of the fathers what a certain solitary did,

> who worked diligently in his garden and gave all that his labor produced as alms and kept for himself only what he needed for his own food. Later, however, Satan put this thought into his heart: Save up a little money, so that, when you are old or get sick, you won't need anything. And he saved up and filled a jar with coins. Now it happened that he took sick and one of his feet began to suppurate. He spent what he had collected on doctors, but it didn't do him any good. Finally one of the medical experts came and told him: Unless your foot is amputated, your whole body will putrefy. So they decided to amputate his foot the next day. But that night he came to his senses and repented of what he had done. He groaned and wept, saying: Remember, O Lord, the deeds I used to do when I worked in my garden and from the proceeds of it helped out the poor. And as he wept, the angel of the Lord stood beside him and said to him: Where are the coins that you collected, and where is the hope that prompted you to act that way? But he responded: Lord, I have sinned. Pardon me; I won't do it any more. Then the angel touched his foot and immediately it was healed. In the morning he got up and went to work in the field. The doctor came with his instruments to amputate his foot. He said: Where is that sick man? They told him: He went out this morning to work in the field. The doctor was amazed and went out and saw him digging up the ground. He glorified God who had given the man back his health.[25]

These words suffice to show how bad it is to save up money after having renounced the world and to hold onto it greedily. That is why it is written: "No one who puts a hand to the plow and then looks back is fit for the kingdom of God" [Luke 9:62].

[25] Ibid., 5.6.21; PL 73:892.

I myself knew a certain brother, and how I wish I did not know him! I could say his name, if it would do any good. Under pretence of religion, he acted as though he were leaving the world and went so far as to lead the solitary life, not in heart, but in body only. Not only did he not distribute absolutely all the possessions and wealth that he once had; he even greedily kept what was offered to him by the faithful. Later the devil put it into his heart that he should go out of the cell in which he had been a recluse so that he could make use of the wealth he had wickedly saved up. And that is what he did. For as long as he lived in the present world, he was a source of scandal, not only to himself, but to all of us. Not only did his example do harm then, but it still injures those who knew him and will harm those who will come to know of him. I say this because there are some who have despised the desires of the flesh and have struggled to leave everything behind, but when they see that that man began the work and then fell, they are afraid to do what they had resolved. Yet these people too must be shown to be wrong. If they are afraid of imitating wicked people in their wickedness, why are they too lazy to imitate good people in their goodness? That is why it is written: "Let us take example from those who are good."[26] The reason why the ruin and undoing of others is written down is so that we might be more concerned about our own life.

Quite enough, I think, has been said about renouncing the world and about not saving up wealth. The next chapters will, with God's help and the assistance of blessed Prosper, speak about the contemplative life.

Chapter 8: What Is Proper to the Active Life, and What Is Proper to the Contemplative Life

Since one comes to the contemplative life by way of the active, I'm afraid that we must first speak of what is proper to the active life. We can then pass on to the contemplative life.

---

[26] Jerome, *Commentarium in evangelium Matthaei*, 4.23; PL 26:181.

The active life is a religious way of living[27] that teaches how superiors should rule those under their care and how they should love them. And since they are concerned for the salvation of their subjects no less than for their own,[28] they are to provide with parental care what they know is for their subjects' good. The active life also teaches how those under a superior should with the greatest love keep to the superior's orders as though they were the command of God, just as bodily members are the dutiful servants of the head.

The life that we are now discussing distributes bread to the hungry, teaches the ignorant with the word of wisdom, corrects the erring, calls the proud back to the path of humility, takes care of the sick. It dispenses to each and all what they need, and it makes sure that those committed to its care have the necessities of life. These things exist with the body in this present time, and they will pass away with the body. Nonetheless, the merit gained by the active life will remain for eternity.

Now this is what the contemplative life is: to hold fast with all one's mind to the love of God and of neighbor, to despise all transitory things, to put visible things behind one and to desire only what is heavenly. The contemplative life derives its name from "contemplating," that is, from seeing. In the contemplative life, a creature endowed with intellect, once purified from every sin, will see its Creator. But if we are willing to concentrate our attention on it, then even in this fragile tent where we daily sigh, we can become to some extent participants in the contemplative life.

Some people think that the contemplative life is nothing else but acquaintance with things hidden and in the future, or leisure from all worldly occupations, or the study of Sacred Scripture. When we visit the sick, bury the dead, and correct the erring, then we are in the active life. But when we shed tears in the sight of God and set ourselves to consider how great is the blessedness, the light, and the glory of the saints in heaven, then we are in the contemplative life. Whereas the active life begins with the body

---

[27] *conversatio religiosa*
[28] See RB 2.39-40.

and finishes here below with it, the contemplative life begins here and reaches fulfillment in the age to come. Of these two lives, the active is signified by Martha, and the contemplative by Mary. But there is no doubt that Mary needs Martha.

Chapter 9: What the Qualities of That Person Should Be in the Active Life Who Is Endeavoring to Rise up to the Contemplative Life

If you are endeavoring to rise up to the peak of the contemplative life, you should first test yourself through many trials in the active life. Can you bear injuries? Can you endure abuse, slander, mockery, insults, and beatings? If you can patiently endure these and similar things, whether they are inflicted by the devil or by another person, then you will someday be able to fly up to the contemplative life. In the active life, all the vices are to be eliminated by the practice of good works, so that in the contemplative life you may with pure attention go on to contemplate God.

Suppose that someone who has just entered the religious life[29] desires to rise immediately to contemplation. That person must nevertheless be compelled by reasoned argument to concentrate first on the exercise of the active life, because whoever first makes progress in the active life afterward is sure to rise up to contemplation. That person deserves to be lifted up to the latter who has been successful in the former. Therefore, those who are still pursuing temporal glory or carnal appetite should be kept from quiet contemplation and instead be purified by the performance of deeds that suit the active life.

It is important to know that holy men went out from the hidden retreat of contemplation to the public sphere of action; then they went back from the observable realm of action to the hidden retreat of intimate contemplation. In the active life, one's intent moves persistently forward, but in the contemplative life one restores one's strength at intervals, because one becomes weary from

---

[29] A *conversus*, a newcomer to the religious life.

contemplation. It is characteristic of the eagle to fix its eye on the sun's ray and not to look aside, except to get food. In the same way, the saints sometimes turn aside from contemplation to the present life. They judge that contemplation is most profitable but that our poverty still needs lowly things a little.

The vision in Ezechiel's prophecy of the living creatures that moved but did not go backward applies to perseverance in the active life. Likewise those living creatures that moved and went backward apply to moderation in the contemplative life. Those who focus on contemplating are beaten back by their weakness and are deflected, but they renew their determination and are once again raised up to the things that they had descended from.

We have said these things by way of preface, so that those who want to live perfectly in the contemplative life must be sure to work with their own hands at set intervals to provide themselves with their livelihood. Still, they must be careful not to seek to gain a living by any dishonest transactions. That is why it is written in Scripture: "No one who serves as a soldier for God gets involved in secular affairs, so that he may please the one who enlisted him" [2 Tim 2:4].

Chapter 10: The Difference between the Active Life and the Contemplative Life

We will now briefly discuss the difference between the active and contemplative lives. That our presentation may be clear and lucid, we will compare the active and contemplative lives, setting out the virtues of each.

It belongs to the active life to make progress in human affairs and to moderate the movements of the rebellious body by the dictate of reason. It belongs to the contemplative life to ascend by the desire for perfection beyond human affairs and constantly to work at increasing virtues. To the active life belongs progress; to the contemplative life, the summit. The first makes holy; the second, perfect. It is characteristic of the active life not to respond to injury with injury; it is characteristic of the contemplative life to bear injuries calmly. Further, if I may add something of my own, those who are living the active life are eager to forgive someone who sins against them; those who pursue the contemplative life are more ready to ignore injuries, as though no blow had been struck at all, than to inflict them.

People living the active life hold anger in check by the virtue of patience and rein in their immoderate desires by the virtue of frugality. They are affected by fleshly desires but do not consent; they are struck by curiosity about the world but are not carried away; they are battered by the devil's instigations but are not overcome. By the devotion of their mind, they subject themselves to their God. They are not terrified by all kinds of temptations but are tested by them. On the other hand, those living the contemplative life overcome by holy virtues all the affections that make the life of mortals so changeable. Free from all desires and distress, they enjoy a blessed quiet. Since by their unencumbered mind they have become superior to every allurement and pleasure, they come to share in the unspeakable joy of divine contemplation.

By taking in pilgrims, clothing the naked, governing subjects, redeeming captives, and protecting victims of violence, those in the active life cleanse themselves from all their iniquities and enrich their life with the fruits of good works. Those in the contemplative life have already given their possessions for the use of the poor and go on to divest themselves of the world and with all their strength withdraw themselves to heaven. They jettison into the world the things of the world and with faithful mind give themselves back to Christ. Like paupers, they pray Christ to give them immortal riches; like the sick, they beg every day to be protected; like the naked, they desire to be clothed with the vesture of immortality; like those oppressed by the weakness of the flesh, they petition to be defended against the attack of invisible enemies; like pilgrims, they desire to be given a heavenly homeland.[30]

The path of the active life is full of cares; the contemplative life, conversely, is the path of eternal joy. In the former we win a kingdom; in the latter we receive it. The former makes a person knock

---

[30] The punctuation of previous phrases in the Holstenius-Brockie text, 299, appears to be confused.

on the door with the hands, so to speak, that are good works; the latter calls those who have been perfected into their homeland. In the former we despise the world; in the latter we see God. Omitting many things that I am unable to mention here, I do say that in the active life, people become stronger than the unclean spirits, whereas in the contemplative life, which is the most blessed, they are rewarded by God and become equal to the angels and are happy and will reign with them for all eternity in that city on high.

Chapter 11: The Contemplative Life Delights, Even Now, Those Who Despise Present Things

Hence, they who sigh for the promised happiness of the contemplative life are those who renounce all present things in favor of the contemplation of future things. They also renounce domestic affairs, which sometimes impede the progress of those who want to live perfectly. Those who are advanced rise above even the desires of their flesh to that height of divine contemplation. They despise within themselves all the things that very often cast souls that until then had been secure in their holiness down to earthly things, and they now approach heavenly things. The closer they get to divine things, the more they ascend in their eagerness for perfection above all human things. They are sure that, if on earth they prefer with their whole will the contemplative life to dubious honors, worrisome wealth, and transitory joys, then God will reward them by having them find true honors, secure wealth, and eternal joys when they reach the perfection of contemplative virtue in that blessed life to come.

Truly, what will be more honorable for the one whom the divine clemency makes blessed with the glory of angelic dignity? What is richer for the one whom the overflowing blessedness of the heavenly reign enriches beyond description? Or what is even here more delightful than divine contemplation, which pours into the person who is truly avid for it the incorruptible sweetness of future reward? Indeed, even here the contemplative life delights those who love it with sight of the good things to come [see Heb 9:11]. It illumines with the gift of spiritual wisdom those who, as far as is possible in this life, free their minds for it and concentrate on nothing else. It inflames them with a kind of drive to attain that fullness of divine vision which those who have set their heart on heavenly things hope to reach. Thus what they now glimpse as a confused reflection and discern only imperfectly they will then behold revealed in all its fullness [see 1 Cor 13:12].

Chapter 12: The Nature and Extent of the Perfection of the Contemplative Life in This Flesh

Finally, if you are pursuing the contemplative life and are eager to be illumined in heart, draw near to your Creator. Devote yourself to him by contemplating and by craving to make him your sole delight. Desire him constantly, and out of love for him flee everything that could turn you away from him. Fix all your thoughts and all your hope on his love. Free yourself for holy meditations on the Sacred Scriptures and take God-given delight in them. Examine your whole self there as though in a shining mirror. As you scrutinize yourself, correct what is distorted, hold on to what is upright, straighten out what is misshapen, cultivate what is beautiful, preserve what is healthy, and strengthen by diligent reading what is sick. Read the precepts of your Lord without tiring, love them beyond words, and fulfill them in practice. Realize that it is they that give you thorough instruction about what to avoid and what to pursue. Persevere in searching out the mysteries of these divine Scriptures. Read about Christ who was promised to you and see him depicted; understand the prophesied destruction of an obstinate people and mourn that it was fulfilled; rejoice at the salvation of the nations; believe both things past, which were predicted and fulfilled, and things to come, which were promised. Stay as far away as possible from the noise of worldly affairs, and so devote all your energies to pondering those things by which you may inflame your whole self[31] with a desire for the reward to come.

---

[31] *animus*

Be intent on spiritual studies by means of which you may daily
become better and more learned.

Love holy leisure, in which you should conduct the business of
your soul. Regard the world as dead as far as you are concerned,
and show that you have been crucified to the world's charms and
allurements. Rank looking upon your Creator as incomparably
superior to delighting in the spectacles of this present life. Keep
making progress and so rise up to the peak of divine contemplation. Never, even for a single moment, turn your gaze away from
the promises to come by looking back to the earth. Constantly fix
your attention on the goal you desire to reach. Put before the eyes
of your soul the blessedness of the life to come and love it.

Do not fear or desire anything temporal, and do not let either
fear of losing some temporal thing or desire for acquiring it weaken
the concentration of your mind. Attractive things should not corrupt you, and hostile things should not unsettle you. Having a good
reputation should not make you puffed up, and having a bad one
should not discourage you. Being falsely accused should not lessen
your joy, nor being praised increase it. Take no joy in temporal
things, and do not mourn over them. In the midst of joys and sorrows, conduct yourself with resolute will.[32] Nothing the world
promises or threatens should shake the steady firmness of your
heart. Instead, persevere in being always the same, always yourself,
and feel neither the injury the world can inflict nor the benefits it
can bestow.

When, in your desire for the contemplative life, you have fulfilled these and similar things, you should be unshakeable in your
belief, not that you have here and now become perfect in every
particular, but that you are being made perfect in that blessed life
that is still to come. You strain forward for the life in which you
will be able to see the substance of God with unveiled face [see
2 Cor 3:18]. In this life people are said to be perfect in comparison
with those who live uprightly, since a just person does the commandments, but a perfect person goes beyond them. In the same

---

[32] *unam faciem animi constantis obtineat*. Here the volitional, steadfast aspect of
animus is in the foreground.

way, if compared to the absolutely perfect ones who will be in that blessed life,[33] perfect people are not, so to speak, perfectly perfect. Even though all their iniquity has been forgiven, still it has not been healed. Rather, their weakness is still being healed. Even though they do not sin and so are truly perfect, yet they are still able to sin because they have not yet been healed, and all their weakness has not yet been done away with. When someone has been cleansed from all sin and can no longer sin, then that person has been totally healed and is completely perfect.

In this life, however, no matter how much a person may stand out by virtue of eminent holiness, no matter how distinguished a person may be because of exceptional perfection, that person can indeed become perfect for a small part of this life but is not thereby safe in that perfection. That person must still experience anxiety about falling. And where there is anxiety, there is not complete blessedness. Blessedness can never be considered perfect if it is not secure, and it will not be secure unless eternal security has done away with all anxiety. And so we see that the blessedness of all the saints will be perfect in that place where human nature will see the glory of its Creator and will cling to him without the slightest defect in blessedness.

Chapter 13: The Saints Cannot See God Perfectly Unless They Have Reached the Blessedness of the Life to Come

It follows from the foregoing that people who desire the contemplative life with all their heart should be exhorted to strive for it, and with God's help they will be able to. But they must remember that the perfection of this divine contemplation has been reserved for them in that blessed life which is to come. When their pursuit of eternal life and of the heavenly kingdom has reached perfection, then they will see God perfectly as he is. Otherwise, if human frailty could contemplate God's substance here perfectly,

---

[33] *absolute perfectis.* Such perfection is absolute because it cannot now be lost or diminished; it has become finalized, impeccable, completed.

the holy Evangelist would never have said: "No one has ever seen God" [John 1:18]. He did not say, "No one will ever see him." Finally, in order to show clearly that the vision of God is not denied to holy people but is delayed, the Lord promises for the life to come what he denies to the present time; he says: "Blessed are the pure in heart, for they will see God" [Matt 5:2]. He does not say that they are seeing God here and now.

Hence, if God, who in this life could not and cannot be seen unless he took on some physical element, will be seen in the life to come, it follows that divine contemplation will reach the perfection we so hope for in the place where all good things will be realized. Consequently, I have not described how sublime the contemplative life will be in the future, where it will be made perfect, in such a way as to deny that it can be attained in this present time by people who despise the world. Such people must be converted and devote themselves entirely to pursuing it. They must be set on fire by their desire and feel only disgust for the charms of the present world. They must become so strong that earthly concerns cannot ensnare them, and they must cling to divine things and to the promises of what is to come. People like this, even in this life, can become sharers in the contemplative life.

Since many things have already been said in the preceding chapters about the contemplative life, what we have said here will suffice, and we can go on to consider what else should be said about the life of solitaries.

Chapter 14: Our Holy Forebears First Began to Live the Solitary Life in Order That They Might Reach the Perfection of the Contemplative Life

Because our forebears of old longed for the homeland on high and desired to enjoy the contemplative life in its perfection, they fled, not only from the way of life led by people of the world, but also from associating with the world. They hid in forests and caves, knowing that the farther they separated themselves from the pleasures of the world, the more the angels would keep them company, and the more they withdrew from this age, the closer they would become to God. They wanted to be physically separated from people of the world, so that they would not somehow become involved in their affairs.

We desire, as far as possible, to follow their example, and if we want to make some progress in the contemplative life, we will strive quickly to separate ourselves from associating with this world. We know that God often protects the life of his elect in the midst of carnal people, but it is quite rare that those who dwell in the midst of worldly pleasures remain unharmed by vices. Even if they are not immediately implicated in them, still they are sidetracked somewhat. If you stay near danger, you will not be able to stay safe for long.

On this point, the conferences of the fathers say: "It is good to flee the world. When a person is next to the world, he is like a man standing by a deep lake. Whenever his enemy wants to, he can easily knock him down into it. But if someone is far from the world, he is like a man dwelling far from a lake. If his enemy tries to knock him down into it, while he is dragging him there by force, God will send him help." [34]

In the same place it also says: "A person who flees from people is like a ripe grape. A person who associates with people, however, is like a sour grape." [35] And it says this also: "The person who loves silence remains impervious to the arrows of the enemy, while the person who mixes in with the multitude receives multiple wounds." [36]

"Blessed Arsenius, while he was still in the palace, feared this association with the world, and so he prayed to the Lord and said: O Lord, direct me to salvation. And immediately a voice came to him saying: Arsenius, flee from people and you will be saved. Later, when he had entered upon monastic life, he again prayed to the Lord the same prayer and said: O Lord, direct me to salvation. And

---

[34] *Vitae patrum*, 5.2.12; PL 73:859.

[35] Ibid., 5.2.10; PL 73:859.

[36] Ibid., 5.2.11; PL 73:859.

again he heard a voice that said to him: Arsenius, flee, be silent, be quiet, for these are the roots of not sinning."[37]

Further, one of the Fathers told this story:

> There were three brothers who were students, and they became monks. One of them chose to reconcile and make peace between people involved in disputes, according to what is written: "Blessed are the peacemakers," and so forth [Matt 5:9]. The second chose to visit the sick, as it is said: "I was sick," and so forth [Matt 25:36]. But the third went away to be quiet in solitude. The first brother, laboring over the disputes of people, got nowhere in his peacemaking. Thus defeated, he went to the brother who was serving the sick and found that he too was discouraged and lacked the power to fulfill the command. The two of them agreed to go to see the brother who had gone away into the desert. They told him their troubles and asked him to tell them what had enabled him to make progress. He kept silent for a little while and then poured water into a cup and said to them: Look into the water. It was all stirred up. And after a little while he said to them again: Now look and see how the water has become clear. And when they peered into the water, they saw their faces, as though in a mirror. Then he said to them: That's how a person is who dwells in the midst of people. Because of the crowd, he doesn't see his own sins. But when he has become quiet, especially in solitude, then he perceives his transgressions.[38]

In this account, we clearly see how much advantage the solitary life offers. It is a kind of racecourse[39] for correcting our way of living. "Whoever sits in solitude," that is, in reclusion, "is snatched away from three wars, namely of hearing, of speaking, and of seeing. Such a person has to battle against only one thing: the thoughts of

---

[37] Ibid., 5.2.3; PL 73:858. Another version of this story is found in 3.190 (col. 802).

[38] Ibid., 5.2.16; PL 73:860.

[39] Latin *stadium*.

the heart." [40] It should be kept in mind that it is much better to live among many people and lead the solitary life than to be in the desert and to nurse the desire in one's mind of being with many people. Indeed worldly people, if they commit some crime in this world, are sent to prison, even though they don't want to go there. Likewise, let us, on account of our sins, take ourselves off to the prison of reclusion, so that, by this voluntary punishing of our mind, we may deserve to be spared the punishments to come. Thus, as the Apostle says: If we pass judgment on ourselves in this age, we will not be judged by the Lord in the age to come [see 1 Cor 11:31].

Chapter 15: Concerning the Procedure for Receiving Brothers into Reclusion[41]

Our Lord Jesus Christ calls everyone into his service, and in his faithfulness and mercy he receives all those who come to him. He calls and receives everyone, because he himself knows who are his, and "he has no need of anyone to testify about human beings, since he knows what is in them" [John 2:25]. But we, who have no way of knowing which people are bad and which are good unless we have tested them, ought to hold to this advice of the Apostle: "Test the spirits to see whether they are from God" [1 John 4:1]. That is why a newcomer to God's service ought first to be thoroughly tested and only later received. This procedure is meant to prevent a person from trying to approach the solitary life with a mind full of pretense and a spirit full of deception.[42] Therefore inquiry should be made into his past life and way of living to see whether he has been temperate in his conduct, chaste in his life, sober, wise, humble,

---

[40] This saying is attributed to Abba Anthony in the *Vitae patrum*, 5.2.2; PL 73:858. With regard to Grimlaicus' wording, see the introduction, "Sources and Style."

[41] In this chapter, Grimlaicus has adapted RB 58, the procedure for receiving newcomers to the monastic life.

[42] *simulata mente ac fallaci animo. Mens* and *animus* are quite similar here; both have to do with the intention of one's actions.

obedient, amiable, instructed in the law of the Lord, careful in giving instruction himself.

When therefore he has been subjected to these and other tests, if he has persevered in knocking and if, after four or five days, it is apparent that he has borne patiently the injuries done him and the difficulty of admission and has remained resolute in desiring what he is requesting, then let his admission be approved either by the bishop or by his abbot. But without the consent of the bishop or of the abbot of the place and also of all the brothers of the monastery in which that brother was formed, the matter is not to be acted upon at all. It should also be prohibited that someone resolve to live this religious way of life in any place other than in communities of cenobites; no one should be allowed to resolve to live in this way in villages or in country churches or in any other places, unless perhaps someone might wish to go apart into the wilderness, as did our forebears of old.

After the bishop or superior of the monastery has granted permission to him to be enclosed, he shall live for one year among the brothers. During this time, he shall not go outside the cloister, except into the church. This testing will show to what extent there are in him the requisite will and stability. If, however, there is a solitary in that monastery or in its environs, then the one who is already tested shall be assigned to test him. If there is no solitary there, a senior shall be assigned to him who is skilled in winning souls and who will submit him to the closest scrutiny and examine whether he really seeks God, whether he is earnest about the work of God, about obedience, prayer, reading, and other things of this sort.

There shall be clearly laid out for him all the harsh and rough things by which one goes to God. And if he promises to persevere in being stable, let this rule be read to him, and let it be said to him: Here, then, is the law under which you want to serve as a soldier; if you are able to serve, go in,[43] but if you cannot, you are free to leave. If he still stands firm, let this rule be read to him carefully, so that he may know what he is entering into, and let him be tested in all patience.

---

[43] *Ingredior* means here both "go in" and "enter upon a service."

If he has thought it over within himself and promises to keep everything, then gently and quietly let him be received into the purpose he has resolved upon, knowing as he does that it is established by the law of the rule that from that day forth he may not go out of that enclosure; neither may he throw off from his neck the yoke of the rule that, during such protracted reflection, he was free either to decline or to accept.[44]

The one who is to be received is to make promise, in the oratory, in the presence of the bishop and all the clergy, with words alone, of his stability and of the conversion of his way of living, before God and his saints, so that if he ever acts otherwise (may it never happen), he may know that he will be condemned by the one he is mocking.

Then that brother is to prostrate himself at the feet of the bishop and of all the brothers assembled around, so that they may pray for him. Let everyone present in that place pray for him, as much as seems proper. If the bishop or abbot so order, let signals be sounded to mark his entry, so that everyone may hear that signal and pray for him.[45]

If he has any possessions, such as those mentioned in previous chapters, either let him distribute them beforehand to the poor or let him confer them by solemn donation on the monastery. He is to keep back nothing of them for himself. He ought to continue wearing the clothes he is entering with, and from then on let him persevere in the solitary life. After he has entered, let the bishop order the door of the cell of reclusion to be sealed with his seal, so that no one will be left in any doubt about the matter. [46]

---

[44] The year in the midst of the cenobitic community has been a kind of novitiate in preparation for the solitary life. In Benedictine fashion, entry into solitude is to be accomplished without display or fuss: *blande leniterque.*

[45] Latin *signa sonent.* Here the "signs" seem to be the ringing of the monastery bell(s), as in RB 48, for example: *facto primo signo nonae horae.*

[46] Some details of this chapter seem to presume that the one entering upon the solitary life is already a monk. He needs neither to sign a vow document nor to receive a habit different from the one he is wearing. In chapter 49, Grimlaicus mentions the clothing of enclosed men who "have not yet taken on the monastic manner of life."

Chapter 16: What the Cell of Reclusion Should Be Like

The cell of reclusion should be small, and it should be surrounded on all sides by very solid walls, so that there be left for the solitary no opportunity for roaming around outside and so that no entry be left open for someone to go in to him, a thing that is not allowed. So that every occasion of having to go out may be thwarted, he shall have rooms inside the enclosure that meet his needs. Thus, he shall have an oratory consecrated by the bishop, if, that is, the solitary is a priest. This oratory should adjoin the church building. In this way, through a window in the oratory, the solitary will be able to offer the sacrifices at Masses through the hands of priests and be able clearly to hear the brothers chanting and reading and be able to sing the psalms along with them. He will also be able to give answers to those who come to him.

A curtain is to be hung in front of this window, both inside and outside, so that he cannot easily be seen from the outside or himself see outside. Otherwise death might be drawn in through the gateway of the eyes, as it is written: Take care that death not enter into your soul through your windows [see Jer 9:21]. And the Apostle orders that people be on their guard against public spectacles and displays.[47]

Within the walls of reclusion he should have a little garden, if it can be arranged, in which he can from time to time go out and plant and collect some vegetables and can get some fresh air, for fresh air will do him a great deal of good.

Outside the walls of reclusion there should also be other little cells in which his disciples live. These cells should be contiguous to his, so that his disciples may have a suitable means of providing him, at the proper time, with the things he needs.

If two solitaries are living in the one place, as is known to be the case in many locations, let there be between them an immense silence, a great quiet, and a perfect charity. The individual solitaries

---

[47] This phrase *spectaculis et pompis praecaveri* does not occur in the Scriptures. Similar wording occurs in Isidore of Seville, *De ecclesiasticis officiis*, 2.2; PL 83:778, where Isidore orders that clerics "not attend public spectacles and displays."

should be separated in individual cells, but they should be insepa-
rably joined together in spirit[48] and in faith and charity. Their cells
should not be separated by a space but so connected to one another
that the solitaries can come to one window and there be able to
encourage one another to serve God, to take time together for the
sacred prayers, to recite together the divine Scriptures, and to come
together at a suitable hour to take bodily sustenance.[49]

As has been said, the cells of solitaries should adjoin the church.
Women are not allowed to take food or to spend time in the cells
of solitaries or in those of their disciples, and they must not even
be provided with any means of entering them, for we read that this
was strictly forbidden by the holy fathers. However, if women need
to speak with the solitaries in order to confess or to take counsel
about their souls, let them come into the church and, in full view
of everyone, let them speak in front of the window that opens on
the oratory, and with prudence and profit, let them confer about
what must be conferred about and resolve it. Just as they do in other
matters, so too in conversing with women, solitaries are obliged to
offer good example to everyone. For instance, their converse with
women should provide no opportunity for anyone to get the wrong
impression. They must refrain, not only from private talks with
women, but also from seeing or touching them. Saint Basil has this
to say about talking with women: "Do not allow your ears to
become accustomed to hearing the words of women, lest from
those words you conceive wickedness in your soul."[50] On this
subject Saint Jerome says: "The chief things that tempt God's servants are the frequent visits of women,"[51] for a female strikes their
conscience with a raging fire and burns up their heart. About

---

[48] Solitaries should be *animo et fide ac charitate inseparabiliter conjuncti.* The one
Latin word, *animus*, here can stand for a whole spectrum of English terms: intention, resolve, mind, heart, spirit.

[49] This window, therefore, is different from the one that opens into the church,
but the same as the one mentioned at the beginning of chapter 17.

[50] Basil, *Admonitio ad filium spiritualem*, 7, as found in the *Codex regularum*; PL
103:689.

[51] This saying is found in a letter attributed to Jerome [Ep 42.2; PL 30:288]
and also in the *Regula Canonicorum* of Chrodegang of Metz, 56; PL 89:1083.

touching women Saint Basil says: "Do not desire to touch a woman's flesh, lest by touching it your heart become inflamed. Just as straw that is close to the fire bursts into flame, so the one who touches a woman's flesh will not get away without harming his soul. Even though he gets away still chaste in body, he will go away wounded in mind and heart." [52] Women should never be kissed by solitaries, because kissing is one of the four forms of physical love. Women are to be loved not carnally but spiritually. But what shall I say about looking at them? The Lord clearly states: "Whoever looks at a woman to desire her has already committed adultery with her in his heart" [Matt 5:28]. That is why Saint Basil says: "Do not look at a woman's shape with a shameless eye, lest by way of the windows of your eyes death enter your soul." [53] And so they must avoid frequently looking at women. This applies especially to those who had lived among seculars or who had been married. They should not be a godparent along with any man or woman. [54] Although it is licit, still it is not good for them.

Chapter 17: There Must Never Be Fewer Than Two or Three Solitaries at a Time

Let every effort be made that, if at all possible, there never be fewer than two or three solitaries at the same time. The solitaries will be enclosed in individual cells, but in such a way that they can speak to each other through a window and will be able to encourage each other to do the work of God. For many reasons, I perceive that the companionship of two solitaries is useful to those who are of the same will and purpose. Conversely, I discern that, for many reasons, to live the solitary life without any company is dangerous. The first danger that threatens solitaries, and it is a very serious one, is that they please themselves and seem to themselves already to have reached the height of perfection and think that they are

---

[52] Basil, *Admonitio ad filium spiritualem*, 7, as found in the *Codex regularum*; PL 103:689–90.

[53] Ibid., 7; PL 103:689.

[54] *compatres quoque et commatres minime faciant*

what they are not. This usually happens to those who do not have anyone with whom their work might be put to the test. About such people the Apostle says: "Those people who think they are something when they are nothing are deceiving themselves" [Gal 6:3]. Furthermore, they will not know whether a given virtue abounds in them or whether it is missing. In addition, since these people are alone, they will not be able to seek from others either what is profitable or what they lack. Finally, they will not easily recognize either their faults or their vices, since there will be no one to admonish and rebuke them. To this kind of solitary can easily happen what is written: "Woe to those left alone, for when they fall, they have no one to lift them up" [Eccl 4:10].

What will prevent solitaries from exercising their wicked desires, if they have no one who might seem to stand in the way of their self-will? Or how will they test their humility or patience or charity, if they have no one toward whom they may exercise these virtues? One person, even the very highest, cannot be sufficient to receive all the gifts of the Holy Spirit, for, as the Apostle says: "Some are given the gift of speaking wisdom, others that of speaking knowledge" [1 Cor 12:8] and other similar passages. If, according to the dispensation of the Holy Spirit, one person is given what another is denied, it follows that there must be two or three or even more, and with the charisms that each of them receives, they may fortify and build one another up.

In addition, the company of several is a great help against the ambushes of the enemy, which are laid both interiorly and exteriorly. They will more easily be roused from sleep and spurred on by every good work. In prayer, too, no small benefit arises from two brothers, especially since the Lord says: "If two of you agree on earth about anything at all that you are praying about, it will be done for you by my Father who is in heaven" [Matt 18:19]. And he also says: "Where two or three have been gathered in my name, there am I in their midst" [Matt 18:20]. Furthermore, two can get through more prayers than one.

A life lived by solitaries in common has many other goods that it is not possible to enumerate now. But in saying that there are two solitaries in one place, we mean that a single one, if that one has been proven, should not be prevented from benefiting from this life.

Chapter 18: Whether Priests from the Surrounding Countryside or Young People Ought to Be Received into the Solitary Life

Since God's kindness calls everyone by means of that most loving call by which he says: "Come to me all you who labor and are burdened, and I will refresh you"[Matt 11:28], the decision to turn away someone who has come to serve God is a perilous one. Nonetheless, it is not without the most careful probation that someone is allowed to enter into this holy way of life. The Lord questioned the young man who came to him about his former life, and when he heard that the young man had behaved uprightly, he commanded him to fulfill what he was lacking and said: "If you wish to be perfect, go and sell all you have and give to the poor" [Matt 19:21], and finally he ordered him to follow him. In the same way, we ought to "test the spirits to see whether they are from God" [1 John 4:1] and so with charity receive into God's service those who come.[55]

If any ordained priest from foreign parts asks to be received, with the intention of coming to the solitary life at some point, he must not be given permission easily. Nevertheless, if he perseveres in requesting it, let him be received. He should know that he is to observe the whole discipline of the rule.[56] But so that someone not turn out to have come to this resolve by pretense only, he is first to be put to a rigorous test. That way it will easily be ascertained whether he carries out with peace of mind all the physical labor that is imposed upon him, and whether he takes easily to an austere life. It can be determined whether, when he is asked, he is not too embarrassed to declare his offense but gladly takes up the remedy

---

[55] RB 58.2 also cites this verse of 1 John in the description of the procedure for receiving newcomers.

[56] See RB 60.1-2, the procedure for admitting priests.

prescribed for him. It can be seen whether he is inclined to be completely humble without feeling demeaned and whether, if the situation requires it, he does not feel ashamed at being assigned to repugnant and menial tasks. When he has been tested by these and other practices, if he has remained stable and shown a ready spirit, then he should be received. But he shall live for two years among the brothers in community, as was said above, and afterward, if his resolution has remained firm, he should be received into the solitary life.[57]

Likewise if a monk on pilgrimage or a cleric from a distant province arrives and asks to be received for the aforesaid reason, he shall be received as a guest and tested in the way already described. If he has been content with the custom of the place as he found it and wants to make his stability firm, his intention should not be denied. If, during the time of his stay as a guest, he has been found to be demanding or corrupt—since during this time it could best be discovered what kind of person he was—not only should he not be received, but he should be frankly told to leave, lest his wretched conduct corrupt others. But if he is not the kind of person who deserves to be expelled, then he should not be expelled but persuaded to stay, so that others may be instructed by his example. Care must be taken that a monk from another known monastery not be received to live in the community without the consent of his abbot or letters of recommendation.[58]

There is no doubt about whether youths should be received or not, since the Lord says of them: "Let little ones come to me, for to such belongs the kingdom of heaven" [Matt 19:14]. Youthfulness does not present an obstacle to a person, provided that person is perfect in mind. Likewise, old age is of no advantage to someone who is a child as regards understanding. Someone is said to be perfect who is so, not in age, but in good sense. That is why it says

---

[57] It seems that those who are not already monks of the monastery at which they seek to be enclosed are to complete a two-year period of testing before being enclosed, rather than the one-year period prescribed for those who are monks of the monastery. See chapter 15.

[58] This paragraph depends on RB 61.

in the book of Wisdom: "Gray hairs are a person's good sense, and old age is a faultless life" [Wis 4:8–9]. We know that David, even though still a boy, possessed perfect understanding, was chosen by the Lord to be king, and was entrusted with the spirit of prophecy. Saul, when he had become an old man, was toppled from the pinnacle of royalty because of his wickedness and was handed over to a malevolent spirit. The priests who tried to violate Susanna were very old, and Daniel who condemned them out of their own mouths was still a boy. When our Lord Jesus Christ entered Jerusalem, he was hailed by children and was later crucified by elders. Likewise a tree, even though it has been growing for very many years, unless it bears fruit, will be cut down, whereas a young tree, if it is productive and fruitful, will be cultivated so that it may produce a more abundant crop [see Luke 13:6ff.].

We state that every time of life, beginning with the first, is the right time to receive people and to instruct them and teach them to fear God. Firm profession of virginity will be made, however, at the time when a person has become an adult, that is, at the age that seculars normally deem appropriate for getting married. Every care, however, must be exercised that they be given the opportunity of putting every virtue into practice. They request entry, as was said above, for the predetermined two years, and if they persevere courageously and fervently, they should be received in the manner set out above.

Furthermore, if someone of the Catholic faith comes to us and says: I want to stay for some time among you to derive profit from you, that person should also be received, as the Lord says: "Everyone who comes to me I will not cast out" [John 6:37]. Meanwhile it can happen that the person makes progress over time and comes to delight in abiding in holiness of life. We must be very careful about the way we live out our religious life, since it is on that basis that people form their different opinions. We should obey the command of the One who said: "Let your light shine before people in such a way that they may see your good deeds and glorify your Father who is in heaven" [Matt 5:16]. This is what should happen: if the visitor is good and truthful, that person may derive profit from us; if inquisitive and deceitful, that person may be confounded.

Chapter 19: What Kind of People and How Holy Solitaries Ought to Be

Solitaries ought to be the kind of people that the Apostle orders a bishop to be: "A bishop ought to be without offense" [Titus 1:7]. Likewise, solitaries ought to be without offense, not impudent, not bad-tempered, not wine-drinkers, not big eaters, not physically violent, not double-tongued, not neophytes, and not avaricious for filthy gain.[59] If we say first of all that solitaries are to be without offense, we do not mean that, if they had committed some offense before their conversion, then they would not be received into the solitary life, since by their very intention, they would be able to do penance for the misdeed they had admitted beforehand. What we mean is that, from the time they begin to dwell in the solitary life, they should not be tormented by any consciousness of sin. The person who has no vices is without offense. Every offense is a sin, but not every sin is an offense. Consequently, a solitary or anyone else can be free from offense but can never be free from sin.[60]

It follows that solitaries ought not to be impudent, that is, proud, lest they become carried away and fall into the devil's trap. They should not be bad-tempered. A bad-tempered person is one who is always getting angry and is stirred by the merest breath of a reply, as leaves are stirred by the wind. Not everyone who gets angry on occasion is bad-tempered. That person is called bad-tempered who is constantly being overcome by this passion.

We say that solitaries must not be wine-drinkers or big eaters, because where there has been drunkenness and overeating, concupiscence and mad desire will have the upper hand. It usually happens that people who are controlled by these two vices offend against sober decorum by raising their voice in laughter and letting out a dirty guffaw through dissolute lips.

They should not be physically violent, that is, they should not be ready to raise their hand to strike. This does not mean that, if a

---

[59] See RB 4.34-38, the tools for good works, and 31.1, the qualities desirable in the monastery cellarer.

[60] Grimlaicus is distinguishing *crimen* (offense, blame, misdemeanor, socially observable misconduct) from *peccatum* (sin).

solitary has a disciple and has been authorized to do so, the solitary may not, out of concern, give the disciple a beating, since Solomon says: The sides of boys are to be given a sound beating with rods, so that they do not become hardened [see Prov 13:24; 23:13-14; 29:15]. But this saying means that people who ought be kind and patient should not lose their temper and lash out at another's mouth or head.

They should not be double-tongued, lest they disturb those who have peace. They should not be neophytes, lest they fall into the devil's trap, since they do not yet know how to guard against the temptations of the enemy. Those who become solitaries at a moment's notice do not know what humility and gentleness are or how to detest the wealth of the world or to despise themselves. They have not fasted or wept or often reproached their own conduct or corrected it by constant meditation. They are carried from throne to throne, from pride to pride.

They should not be avaricious for filthy gain, lest they seek to win earthy gain from God's service. Avarice for filthy gain means thinking more about present things than about things to come. Solitaries have food and clothing, and with these they ought to be content. That is why the Apostle says: Those who serve the altar should live from the altar [see 1 Cor 9:13]. He says "live," not get rich.

They should not be irritable and anxious, should not go to extremes or be obstinate, should not be jealous or overly suspicious, because this sort of solitary will never have rest. They should not be given to grumbling, since it is written that those who grumbled were destroyed by serpents [see Jdt 8:24-25; Num 21:5-6; and 1 Cor 10:9].

They should not disparage others, because of what is written: The one who disparages brother or sister will be wiped out [see Jas 4:11]. They must not harbor hatred in their heart, for it is written: "The one who hates brother or sister is a murderer" [1 John 3:15]. They must not be empty talkers, for it is written: "Every idle word that people speak, they will account for on the day of judgment" [Matt 12:36].

They must not be lazy, because of what is written: "You bad and lazy servant," and so on [Matt 25:26]. They should not be sleepy or subject to any other vices, so that they can be confident and dare to say with the prophet: "I will be spotless before God and will hold myself back from my iniquity [Ps 17:24].

Thus far we have been showing what sort of people the servants of God should not be. Now let us say what sort of people they should be. The servants of God ought to be modest, that is, they keep themselves in check and free from lust. As I have said, they should stand out among others, not just because they abstain from actions that would make them impure, but because their mind is free from wandering thoughts.

They should be just, holy, and chaste. They should practice abstinence and hospitality and love good works. They should be modest, serious, patient, kindly, humble, charitable, and obedient. Not only should they abstain from immoral acts, but they should also keep themselves free from impulses of eye, word, and thought. This is the kind of people they should become: even as they allow no vice to dominate them, they are able to beg God for pardon for their own wicked deeds and those of all people.

Furthermore, solitaries should live in such a way that those who disparage religion do not dare to disparage their life. If they are this kind of people and pursue the virtues mentioned above, then they will be profitable ministers of God and, with the help of divine mercy, will bring their resolve to perfect completion.

Chapter 20: How Solitaries Should Be Taught, and in What Manner They Should Teach Others, and How They Should Discretely Look after One Another

Solitaries ought to be teachers, not people who need to be taught, and they ought also to be wise and learned in the divine law and thus know from what source they may bring forth things both new and old [see Matt 13:52].

There are many reasons why solitaries must be instructed in the divine utterances. First, on account of the wiles and trickery that the devil often uses to bore into the hearts of senseless people. Second, so that they may be able to water with the flowing streams of doctrine the parched hearts of those neighbors who come to

them. And if they have some disciples, they should be able to instruct them sufficiently. In these and similar situations, it is absolutely necessary that solitaries know the Scriptures, because, if their
holy life touches only themselves, then the fact that they live in a
holy manner will benefit them alone. But if they are learned in
doctrine, then they will be able to instruct others and to rebut and
refute heretics and Jews and other kinds of adversaries. Unless these
are refuted and shown to be wrong, they can easily corrupt the
hearts of simple people.

The speech of solitaries, however, ought to be pure, simple, and
open, full of dignity and honesty, full of sweetness, grace, and gentleness. It is their special duty to explain the mystery of the Law, the
doctrine of the faith, the virtue of self-control, and the discipline
of justice; to read the divine Scriptures, to peruse the canons, to
imitate the examples of the saints in order to know beforehand
what they should bring forth, to whom, when, and how they
should speak of it. One and the same advice should not always be
given to everyone, but each person should receive different counsel,
depending on the nature of that person's conduct and state in life.[61]
It takes a firm reprimand to correct some people, while a mild
reprimand corrects others. Just as expert physicians use various
medicines to suit the various kinds of wounds, so solitaries ought
to apply to individual people an appropriate remedy of advice.
They should declare to each person what is appropriate for that
one's age, sex, and state in life. Not everything that is hidden should
be revealed. That is to say, there are many people who cannot grasp
such things. Especially to ignorant and carnal people, what is
preached should be simple and common matters, not the most
exalted and difficult to understand. That is why the Apostle says:
"I was not able to speak to you as to spiritual people, but as to
carnal. As though to babies in Christ I gave you milk to drink, not
solid food" [1 Cor 3:1-2]. In speaking to carnal souls, as we have
said, one must not speak either about the lofty things of heaven or
about earthly things, but rather in ordinary language and with

---

[61] *juxta professionis morumque qualitatem. Professio* here, as below, probably refers
to a person's state in life, whether lay, clerical or religious, married or single.

discretion. Crows, while they see that their chicks are white, do not feed them but only begin to care for them when they turn black like their parents. Then they nourish them with frequent feedings. It is the same for resolute solitaries: unless they see that the people they are advising are, by confessing and doing penance, turning black so as to resemble them and are putting aside the white color of the world and are putting on, by remembrance of sin, the habit of lamentation, it is not good for them to open up to them the more profound mysteries of spiritual understanding, for fear that they will not grasp what they hear and instead begin to despise the celestial precepts before they learn to revere them. For this reason, the Lord says, among other things: "Do not set pearls in front of pigs, lest perhaps they trample them with their hoofs" [Matt 7:6].

Thus far, then, we have been speaking about how learned and how discerning in teaching solitaries must be. Now let us turn to the pronouncement of blessed Gregory and see with what discretion and circumspection we ought to look to ourselves when we teach. He says:

> Because we are weak human beings, when we speak to people about God, we ought first to remember what we are, so that we may reflect on our own fragility and so determine the sequence we should follow in teaching our brothers and sisters. And so let us consider either that we are like some of the people we are correcting or that we have at one time been like them. And if, thanks to the working of God's grace, we are not now like them, we should correct them the more gently and with a humble heart the more clearly we recognize that we too were once involved in these shameful deeds. Even if we are not now and never were like those people still are whom we are hoping to correct through penance, we should watch out that our heart does not become proud of our own innocence and so plunge into a worse ruin than the people whose evil deeds we are correcting. Further, we should call before our eyes other deeds of theirs which were good. If there are none of these at all, then let us have recourse to God's hidden judgments. Just as we have received the good that we

do through no merits of our own, so the grace of heavenly
virtue can pour into them and so arouse them that they may
afterward excel even those goods that we have previously
received. With these thoughts, then, we should first humble
our heart and only then rebuke the sinful deeds of wrong-
doers.[62]

We should realize that it is fitting for bishops and priests to
preach in one way, and solitaries in another. The responsibility of
the former is to preach to the people who are, as it were, committed to their care by accusing, rebuking, and appealing [see 2 Tim
4:2].[63] Solitaries do not have people committed to them, but it is
their task, moved by love alone, to nourish those who come to
them with a banquet of spiritual words and humbly and privately
to inspire people to serve God and so be converted. They must
take care not to restrain the rigor of their exhortation with a view
to gaining human favor. Furthermore, we ought to preach every
day by keeping silence, and we will preach by keeping silence when
we show others how to live well and put before them examples of
light.

Chapter 21: Solitaries Should Give All People Examples of Light, and They Should Live Praiseworthy Lives but Should Not Seek to Be Praised.

The life and conduct of solitaries ought to take its norm and
example from the Apostle, who said: "I have become all things to
all people, so that I may win all" [1 Cor 9:22]. The Apostle pre-
sented himself for everyone's imitation even to the extent of crying
out with self-assurance: "Be imitators of me, just as I am of Christ"
[1 Cor 11:1]. O how fortunate, how confident about his conduct
was Paul, who passed over the prophets and apostles and the other
saints and ordered Christians to imitate him! That is why solitaries,
even though they are inferior to Paul, should nevertheless present

---

[62] Gregory the Great, *Moralia in Hiob*, 23.13; PL 76:266.
[63] See also RB 2.23.

themselves to everyone to be imitated. For, just as it is a valuable and wonderful thing to act well in the midst of the multitude and to inspire many people to make progress and imitate an example of good works, so too it is a dangerous and destructive thing to act negligently and so to shatter the faith and corrupt the souls of many. I say this because unfortunately it is easier to find people who chase after what is inferior than to find those who follow what is better. Consequently, just as that person is to be greatly admired and praised whose good course of life leads many to make progress, even so that person is rightly to be lamented whose life is the ruin of many. Hence, many solitaries who lead corrupt lives act for others a pattern for evil, whereas they should be an example of how to live good lives. Solitaries who cause the ruin of others by the example of their bad conduct will doubtless perish together with them for all eternity, but only if they have persevered in evil. Those who by their example or teaching corrupt the life and conduct of good people are far worse than those who ravage the possessions and estates of others. The latter take away things that are external to us even though they belong to us, whereas those who corrupt conduct destroy our very selves, since the wealth of people is their conduct.

On this account, we who aspire to lead the solitary life must devote our energy always to doing what will build others up. We must be careful that our vices not harm the virtues of others, that our tepidity not weaken the fervor of others, that our anger not stain and our rancor not violate or defile the patience of others, that our pride not corrupt the humility of others, that our sickness not infect the health of others, that our decay not contaminate the beauty of others, that we not extinguish the burning lamps of others, that (may it never happen) we not be excluded with the foolish virgins from the kingdom of God [see Matt 25:1-13].

On the contrary, let us show ourselves to be the kind of people whose humility confounds the pride of others, whose patience extinguishes the rancor of others, whose obedience silently rebukes the laziness of others, whose fervor spurs to action the tepidity of others. Further, let us show ourselves to be the kind of people who are an example of light for everyone. This is what the Lord commands, when he says: "Let your light shine before people in such a way that they may see your good deeds and glorify your Father who is in heaven" [Matt 5:16]. And that is why Saint Paul says: "In everything, therefore, present yourself as an example of good works" [Titus 2:7], "in word, in conduct, in love, in faith, in chastity" [1 Tim 4:12]. On this account, Gregory the excellent teacher says, in his exposition of Ezekiel: "Those who live well in secret but do not contribute to the progress of others are coal. But those who are so placed that their holiness may be imitated and who give off the light of uprightness are lamps, because they both burn for themselves and give light to others."[64] Gregory also says: "Those who shun having others know about their lives are on fire for themselves but do not act as examples of light for others. Those, however, who propose an example of the virtues and who manifest light to others by a life of good works and the word of preaching are rightly called lamps."[65] For this reason, blessed Jerome says: "A harmless way of living that is without speech is as harmful by silence as it is beneficial by example."[66] Thus it is abundantly clear that we ought to be an example to all in both our conduct and our speech.

Nonetheless solitaries must take great care to live praiseworthy lives but not seek to be praised, lest that very praise cause them to fall into conceit and vainglory. If they are not to go to their ruin by the pestilential vice of vainglory, they must always keep in their heart the example of the Apostle: "Whoever glories should glory in the Lord" [1 Cor 1:31], and also: "If it is appropriate to glory, it will do no good" [2 Cor 12:1]. I say this because it seldom happens that those who are living a praiseworthy life are not seized by human praise and carried off by vainglory. Solitaries, therefore, must strive always to present themselves as examples of people who are dying to all fleshly vices, who live spiritually, and who despise vainglory.

[64] Gregory the Great, *Homiliae in Hiezechihelem*, 1.5.6; PL 76:823.
[65] Ibid.
[66] Jerome, Ep 69.8; PL 22:663.

Chapter 22: Those Who Can Be Put in Charge of Governing but Who Flee from Being in Charge because They Wish to Live a Life of Peace

There are some who have been endowed with great gifts of wisdom and learning and who burn with a desire to devote themselves exclusively to contemplation. They flee from having to serve their neighbors' advantage by preaching; they love a secret place of quiet and crave the retreat of contemplation. If, when they have been called to assume a position of leadership, they decline, then clearly they are very often depriving themselves of the gifts that they received not only for themselves but also for others. Since these people are thinking of their own advantage and not that of others, they are doubtless guilty of depriving the community of the gifts they could have brought with them. By what reasoning do they who might shine and benefit others prefer their solitary retreat, when the highest Father's Only-begotten himself willed to benefit the many and went forth from the Father's bosom for the common good of us all? Finally, Truth itself says to his disciples in the Gospel: "A city set on a mountain cannot be hidden" [Matt 5:14], and also: "No one lights a lamp and puts it under a bushel basket but on a lampstand, so that it may give light to all who are in the house" [Matt 5:15]. For this reason he says to Peter: "Simon, son of John, do you love me?" And when Peter immediately responds that he loves him, he hears: "If you love me, feed my sheep" [John 21:17]. If therefore the proof of love is that one cares for the flock, whoever has virtues in abundance yet declines to pasture God's flock is convicted of not loving the Supreme Shepherd.

> If we take care of our neighbor as we do ourselves, we are, as it were, protecting both feet with sandals.[67] Conversely, those who think only of their own good and neglect that of their neighbors are like someone who disgraces himself by losing the sandal of one foot. There are some people who, out of

[67] In his discussion about assuming authority, Gregory cites Deut 25:5-10 and Eph 6:15, both of which passages mention feet and sandals.

humility alone, refuse to be put in charge of others; they do not want to be set over those whom they consider superior to themselves. The humility of such people—presuming that it is joined to the other virtues—will be true in God's eyes if it is not obstinate in rejecting what it is advantageous to undertake. Neither are those people truly humble who discern the indication of God's will that they should be in charge and who nevertheless refuse. Since the position of leadership is enjoined upon them, and especially if they are known to have gifts by which they could both be in charge of others and profit them,[68] they should flee from their own heart and reluctantly obey.[69]

Thus far the words of blessed Gregory.

On this same topic Saint Isidore says:

A man of the church ought to be crucified to the world through the mortification of his flesh, and if he is promoted by God's will, he should also undertake, unwillingly to be sure but humbly, the governance of the ecclesiastical order. Satan ambushes with many ruses those who are eminent by their lives of good sense and by their usefulness to others but yet do not want to have authority over others and be of profit to them. Even though the guidance of souls is imposed upon them, they refuse and think that it is more advantageous to lead a life of leisure than to devote themselves to the advantage of souls. Nonetheless they are deceived and are acting as the devil has persuaded them; he has fooled them by an appearance of good. Because the devil has removed them from the pastoral office, they will never profit those people who could have been taught by their words and example.[70]

---

[68] This phrase, *et prodesse*, with its reference to RB 64:8, was added by Grimlaicus.

[69] Gregory the Great, *Regula pastoralis*, 1.5, 1.6; PL 77:19–20.

[70] Isidore of Seville, *Sententiarum libri*, 3.33.1-2; PL 83–705.

Chapter 23: About the Life and Behavior of Solitaries and How They Ought to Conduct Themselves in the Solitary Life

The blessed apostle Paul is concerned, if I may speak this way, about our life and conduct and admonishes us like a father and says: "Look to your call," and so on [1 Cor 1:26]. The reason we should look to our call is this: our striving for the solitary life will do us little or no good if we are in it as we were in the world. To come to the solitary life is the height of perfection, but not to live perfectly in solitude is the depth of damnation. What good is it to hold onto a quiet place with the body only and to have disquiet dwelling in one's heart? What good is it, I say, to have silence in a house while those who live there are beset by the tumult of the vices and the contention of the passions? What good is it if serenity holds sway over our exterior and a hurricane rages within?

We did not come to the solitary life so that we might enjoy everything in abundance in perfect quiet. We came here, not for rest or security, but for struggle; we sallied forth to do combat; we hastened out to make war on the vices.[71] Our vices are our enemies. But we must be careful never to make a treaty with them. It is imperative that we be ceaselessly on guard and keep careful watch, because this enemy will never make peace. It can be conquered but can never be taken into friendship. This battle, then, that we have taken up is extremely strenuous, extremely hard, extremely dangerous, because it is waged within a human being and is over only when that human life is over. Therefore we have come to this tranquil, hidden and spiritual life to contend every day against our passions by tirelessly attacking them and so circumcise the wickedness of our heart and blunt the sword of our tongue.

We want to erect a tall tower. Let us get ready the resources we need to build with, so that we may complete the building that we started, lest we become a laughingstock to passers-by, and our enemies gloat over us and say: They began to build but could not finish [see Luke 14:30]. May the Lord avert this taunt from us. This tower

---

[71] This description of the solitary life echoes that of RB 1.5.

is not constructed out of stones but out of virtues of the soul. It needs resources, not of gold and silver, but of a faith-filled way of living.[72] Indeed earthly wealth very frequently gets in the way of this construction. For it is hard to serve two masters, and those who serve mammon cannot carry spiritual weapons. No, they will take off Christ's easy yoke and throw it away, and what is heavy and burdensome to their souls will seem to them easy and light [see Matt 11:28-30]. Solitaries of that kind are wounded by their own weapons, and since they love danger, they tumble down into death.

If we, for our part, desire to wage war for God, we should serve him alone and put earthly wealth behind us. It is the special mark of our profession that we seek for no sort of honor in this life but get ourselves[73] ready for what is promised as our eternal reward, that we rejoice in being subject to others and in being thought good for nothing, that we embrace voluntary poverty and eradicate from our hearts not only possessions, but even the desire for them, since it does a person no good not to have riches and still to be possessed by the desire to have them. We should have, not as much as our cravings desire, but only as much as we need. The desire to possess, if it is not entirely cut off, burns more fiercely in small matters and is most tormented about the least things.

There is another case that is extremely serious and lamentable, namely, when one focuses all one's effort on something and does not receive the fruit of that effort. What good is it to fast and keep vigil but not correct one's behavior? It is as though someone were to weed and cultivate outside and around a vineyard but leave the vineyard itself barren and untilled so that thorns and thistles sprang up there. Or what good does it do to afflict the body if we are defiled by the wicked and disparaging remarks of the tongue, as the Apostle says: "If people think they are religious and do not rein in their tongue but deceive their heart, their religion is worthless" [Jas 1:26]. Doesn't all our effort vanish like smoke and shade? Doesn't it disintegrate into nothing like the ash of tow? That's why it is useless for us to flatter ourselves that we crucify the body and

---

[72] *conversatione fideli*

[73] *animum praeparare. Animus* here refers to the whole self.

torment the heart, if our outer self, that is, our body, is engaged in holy labors while our inner self is not cured of passions, that is, detraction, anger, resentment, hypocrisy, and vices of this sort. A solitary like this seems to me to be like someone who made a statue that was gold on the outside but mud on the inside, or like a splendid and expertly constructed house that was painted on the outside with the most beautiful colors but was full of snakes and scorpions inside. About such people Christ says in the Gospel: "Woe to you hypocrites, who are like whitened tombs that on the outside seem lovely to people but on the inside are full of hypocrisy and wickedness" [Matt 23:27, 28]. Just before this, the Lord himself, like a devoted physician, gives us who are sick this advice: "First clean what is inside the cup and dish, so that what is outside may become clean, too" [Matt 23:26], that is to say, first clean your heart of all hypocrisy and wickedness, of all anger and detraction, and then your work will be bright all over without the slightest trace of darkness.

Chapter 24: On the Same Topic as the Previous Chapter

Let us be certain, as indicated by the saying of our Lord cited above, that, unless we are every day on guard against our passions and besiege them, we will become much worse than we were while we lived in the world, and our last state will be worse than our first [see Matt 12:45]. For this reason we must not only guard ourselves against capital sins but must also spit out every day those little acts of negligence as though they were the devil's venom. Just as drops of water leak into a ship's hold through the tiniest cracks, so do the smallest sins leak into our souls every day. A ship that has escaped the waves of the deep will be filled by the tiniest drops and sink, if it has not been bailed out in port. That is how it is with solitaries who have defeated and overcome the dangerous waves that are the offenses of this world. If, when they have arrived at the harbor of solitude, they neglect to bail out from the hold of their soul the minute sins committed on impulse, they will run the danger of suffering shipwreck in the very harbor of quiet.

But someone will say: How can the soul be bailed out? This is how: by praying, keeping vigil, fasting, abstinence, confessing those sins, and by showing genuine charity, genuine humility, genuine patience. Even though solitaries be just and holy, they will never be absolutely safe in this life, because, as the Scripture says: "People do not know whether they are worthy of love or of hate, but all things are kept uncertain in the future" [Eccl 9:1-2]. Many snares are still spread out to catch our feet. It is as though someone were crossing over a river on a very narrow bridge. He thinks he has avoided the worst of the danger by making no misstep. But if, when he comes to the last stretch of the bridge, he loses his balance even a little, then he can meet with the fall that he was fearing while in the middle of the bridge. So it is with us. Even if it seems that we have gotten through the greater part of this life with no mishap, we must not presume to be confident, since the final part of danger still lurks. Therefore we should not judge that we are safe until we have arrived at life's end and brought it to a successful completion. What good is it if a vineyard in blossom fills me with every hope, but then, because wild animals wreck it or hail devastates it, dashes all my hope at harvest time?

That is why all success, all labor that aims at happiness, is embodied in the end. To keep us from slackening our efforts because we feel too safe, the saying of the Lord against mediocrity may be cited that says: "Would that you were hot or cold! Now, however, because you are tepid, I am going to vomit you out of my mouth" [Rev 3:15-16]. It is as though he were saying: You would have done better to have stayed in the world and been cold than to be tepid in the solitary life. Now, however, because you have withdrawn from the world and have, through your negligence, not wanted to take hold of spiritual fervor, you have become tepid and are on the point of being spit and vomited out of the Lord's mouth. And so it is essential that we pay close attention to that saying of the divine Scripture that says: "With all watchfulness preserve your heart" [Prov 4:23].

We are all bound, therefore, to examine and scrutinize each other's deeds every day to see who of us is more eager to perform the work of God, who is more fervent in prayer, more careful in reading, purer in chastity, more profuse in shedding tears, more decorous in body, more sincere in heart; who is kinder in anger, more modest in gentleness, less ready with laughter, more fervent in compunction, more steadfast in seriousness, more joyful in charity. In this way, let us daily render an account to one another of our way of living[74] and say: Let us see whether we have spent this day without sin, without envy, without grumbling, without anger, without slander. Let us see whether today we have accomplished anything that contributes to our own progress and to the edification of others. Let us see whether today we have indulged in more laughter, more food or drink, more rest or sleep than is appropriate. Let us see whether we have read or have prayed less than we ought.[75] In so doing, let us feel remorse on our beds for all our transgressions [see Ps 4:5], that is, in our hearts. And if God grants that we glimpse anything good in ourselves, let us render thanks to the One from whom every good thing comes. If, on the other hand, we discover anything vicious in us (may it never happen), let us attribute it to ourselves and hurry anew to repent.[76]

The things that we have just briefly outlined apply generally to all solitaries, and not only to them, but also to all God's servants and to all Catholic Christians. In addition, if two solitaries are living in the same place, as has been said above, they must not grow listless in leisure or spend their time spreading lies about others and telling obscene stories. Rather, they should devote themselves to chanting the psalms, to spiritual readings,[77] and, of course, to working with their hands. They are to observe the canonical hours with all devotion and in them fulfill the Divine Office. As soon as the signal is given, they should go to their own oratory. Every day they should come to confer together[78] and discuss God's service and their common progress and beg pardon of each other for their faults.

---

[74] *de conversatione nostra*

[75] The foregoing echoes RB 49.1-7, which deals with the observance of Lent.

[76] See RB 4.42-43.

[77] Grimlaicus has the plural, *divinae lectiones*, of the traditional term, *lectio divina*, for the meditative reading of the Scriptures, the fathers, and other spiritual writings.

[78] *ad collationem simul veniant. Collatio* in early monastic writings often refers to a gathering of persons, either with or without discussion. "Come to confer together" tries to catch both senses.

If a solitary is living entirely alone, he too must confer every day with himself. Every day he is to sit down on the judgment seat of his mind and stand himself in his own sight. Thus he is to set up a court in his heart in which thought is the prosecutor, conscience the witness and fear the executioner. The blood of the confessing soul should flow out through tears. Finally let him judge himself in conscience to be unworthy and a sinner. This much about a single solitary.

If, as has been said, there are two solitaries, they must humbly show honor to each other. The junior by birth is to reverence the one who is senior in age in deference to his holiness. In turn, the senior must train the junior how to live well by word and example. Someone from a noble family must not think that he is better than someone who is not of the nobility. Let him know that "God shows no partiality" [Rom 2:11].[79] Likewise, someone who has mastered the knowledge of doctrines and is expert in other good works must not think that he is better anyone else. No, he must thank God for the gifts bestowed on him by God and always weigh what the Apostle says: "If you think you are standing, take care lest you fall" [1 Cor 10:12]. Jerome has this to say: "We should fear and beware lest a storm that lasts only one hour destroy our former glory and sturdy firmness."[80]

Because they are duty bound to show charity, they should humbly anticipate each other. They should stoop down to take care of each other's weaknesses and provide for each other's needs. Every day, if the locality is suitable, they should take turns providing each other with both spiritual and bodily food. They should share one prosperity, and likewise, if need be, one adversity. The will of one should give way to the will of the other. Both of them should submit their wills to the will, or rather, to the servitude, of God. They should do, not what one of them by himself wants, but what both decide on. They should always remember that saying of the Lord: "I have not come to do my own will but that of the Father who sent me" [John 6:38].

---

[79] See RB 2.20 where Rom 2:11 is also quoted. Here Grimlaicus differs from Benedict, for whom age must never determine seniority. See RB 63.

[80] Jerome, *Commentarium in Ezechielem*, 8.26; PL 25:245.

Chapter 25: The Tools of Good Works

The pages of all the holy Scriptures are filled with tools of good works, and throughout the fields of those same holy Scriptures can be found weapons with which the vices may be restrained and the virtues nourished. Nonetheless it is necessary that we introduce into this rule the discourse of a certain father on the tools of good works. In it is contained, in very succinct form, what solitaries should do and what they should avoid.[81]

Solitaries are bound

1. first of all to love God with one's whole heart, whole soul, and whole strength,

2. next, to love one's neighbor as oneself,

3. next, not to kill, that is, not to slander, for, as the Apostle says: Whoever slanders a brother or sister is a murderer [see 1 John 3:15],

4. next, not to commit adultery,

5. not to steal,

6. not to covet,

7. not to bear false witness,

8. to honor all people [see 1 Pet 2:17],

9. and what one does not want someone to do to oneself, one should not do to another,

10. to deny oneself to follow Christ,

11. to chastise the body,

12. not to embrace pleasures,

13. to love fasting,

14. to refresh poor people,

15. to clothe the naked,

---

[81] The remainder of this chapter, except for an excursus between items 17 and 18, is taken almost verbatim from RB 4.

16. to visit the sick,

17. to bury the dead.

We must ask how a solitary can visit a sick person or someone in prison, or bury the dead, since he has no way of leaving his cell. Without a doubt, that person visits someone who is sick or in prison who sees someone lying on a bed or in the darkness of the vices and laboring under the disease of his wickedness. By means of the procedures that are his example and by the antidote that is his wholesome counsel, he strengthens the person he sees stumbling and getting weaker in doing good works. That person buries the dead who faithfully and constantly pours out to the Lord prayers for the one who has died. But not only does he bury someone who has died, but, if I may say so, he also raises him from death: he sees a person entangled in the snares of his sins and entombed, as it were, in the darkness of his wickedness; he rouses him by earnestly counseling him to confess his sins and to repent of them with weeping, and he urges him with healthful advice to return to the path of salvation. On this account we should realize that there is greater merit in raising sinners from vice than there is in raising a dead person from the tomb.

The list continues:

18. to assist in trouble,

19. to console the sorrowing,

20. to make oneself a stranger to the deeds of the world,

21. to put nothing before the love of Christ,

22. not to put anger into action,

23. not to nurse bad temper,

24. not to hold deceit in the heart,

25. not to give a false peace,

26. not to abandon charity,

27. not to swear on oath, lest perhaps one forswear oneself,

28. to utter truth with heart and mouth,

29. not to render evil for evil,

30. not to injure anyone but to endure patiently an injury done,

31. to love enemies,

32. not to curse those who curse one, but rather to bless,

33. to endure persecution for the sake of justice,

34. not to be proud,

35. not to get drunk on wine,

36. not to overeat,

37. not to sleep too much,

38. not to be lazy,

39. not to grumble,

40. not to slander,

41. to put one's hope in God,

42. to attribute whatever good one sees in oneself to God, not to oneself,

43. but one knows that the evil is always done by oneself, and one attributes it to oneself,

44. to fear the day of judgment,

45. to be in dread of Gehenna,

46. to desire eternal life with all spiritual yearning,

47. to hold death daily up to view before one's eyes,

48. to keep guard at every hour on the actions of one's life,

49. in every place to know for certain that God sees one,

50. to smash against Christ the bad thoughts that come into one's heart,

51. and to reveal them to a spiritual senior,

52. to guard one's mouth against bad or degenerate talk,

53. not to love to speak much,

54. not to speak pointless words or words that cause laughter,

55. not to love much or excessive laughter,

56. to listen willingly to holy reading,

57. to devote oneself often to prayer,

58. every day to confess to God in prayer with tears and sighs the evil things one once did and from then on to correct those bad deeds,

59. not to carry out the desires of the flesh: to hate one's own will,

60. to obey the orders of the seniors in everything, even if—may it never happen—they do otherwise, and to remember that precept of the Lord: "Do what they say, but do not do what they do" [Matt 23:3],

61. not to want to be called holy before one is, but first to be so, that it may be said more truly,

62. every day to fulfill God's commandments with deeds,

63. to love chastity,

64. not to hate anyone,

65. not to harbor jealousy or envy,

66. not to love controversy,

67. to flee from self-exaltation,

68. to reverence the seniors,

69. to love the juniors,

70. in the love of Christ to pray for one's enemies,

71. to make peace before sunset with those with whom one is quarreling,

72. and never to despair of God's mercy.

These are the tools of the spiritual craft. If we put them to use day and night in a way that cannot be put into words[82] and turn them in on the day of judgment, the Lord will reward us with the wages that he promised: "What eye has not seen nor ear heard, what has not entered into the human heart—the things that God has prepared for those who love him" [1 Cor 2:9]. Now the workshop where we are to work at all these things is the cloister, that is to say, the cells of solitaries, and stability in reclusion.

Chapter 26: Observing God's Commandments

It is incumbent on all Christians, and especially on solitaries, to observe and obey the commandments of our Lord Jesus Christ. But we should realize that what helps us even more to be mindful of God and to obey his precepts is to live a very hidden and isolated life. Living mixed in with those who act as though they cared nothing for the fear of God and who treat his commandments with contempt is very harmful, as Solomon testifies when he says: Do not dwell with the irreligious, lest perhaps you learn their ways and fashion snares for your soul [see Prov 22:24-25 and Sir 37:12], and also: "Do not emulate the unjust, lest you imitate their ways" [Prov 3:31]. And this is why Peter the apostle says: Therefore it is just, entirely just, to separate the one who wants to be saved from the one who does not.[83] Likewise, Paul speaks this solemn pronouncement: "We make this pronouncement to you, brothers and sisters, by the coming of our Lord Jesus Christ, that you withdraw yourselves from any brother or sister who is walking in disorderly fashion" [2 Thess 3:6]. On this topic, Jerome says: "Avoid like the plague the cleric turned businessman, the poor person become rich, the low-born become prominent, for vile conversation corrupts good conduct [see 1 Cor 15:33]. You despise gold; that other person loves it. You tread on wealth; the other pursues it. You have set your heart on gentleness, silence, and seclusion; the other on

---

[82] Our text has *ineffabiliter* whereas RB 4.76 has *incessabiliter*, ceaselessly.

[83] It is not clear to which scriptural passage Grimlaicus is referring. See 2 Pet 2:7-8 and Matt 13:49.

talkativeness."[84] This is sufficient to show that it is very harmful when people who lead disparate lives associate and intermingle.

So then, since we do not want to receive, by way of our eyes or our ears, bad enticements to sin, and since we want to be able to devote ourselves freely to prayer, we have to live completely hidden and solitary. By this means we will be able to cut off from ourselves the habits we have mentioned above by which we used to act contrary to God's commandments. Indeed, it is no small labor to turn oneself aside and call oneself back from a former bad habit. That is why the common proverb says: A bad habit is hardly ever, or even never, removed. Consequently, if we want to observe and keep God's commandments, let us make every effort first of all to deny ourselves, take up Christ's cross, and so follow him [see Matt 16:24]. The Lord himself challenges us to love him and observe his commandments when he says: "If you love me, keep my commandments" [John 14:15]. And he also says: "Whoever has my commandments and keeps them, that is the one who loves me" [John 14:21]. We love God only if we keep his commandments and despise all visible things for love of him. Conversely, we do not love God at all if we do not keep his precepts. Thus the apostle John says: Whoever says: I love God, yet does not keep his commandments, is a liar [see 1 John 4:20; 2:4]. Unquestionably, we love God if we observe his commandments. It is in carrying out his commandments that we can know whether we love God or not.

We have not here taken up the commandments of Christ in order and gone into every detail; rather, we have treated them only in part and only insofar as is necessary for our purpose and the present discussion demands. The whole can be understood from the part. First, then, we must consider the things that may prompt us to love God and neighbor, that is, "You shall love the Lord your God with all your heart and with all your mind and with all your strength. This is the greatest and first commandment. The second is like it: You shall love your neighbor as yourself. On these two commandments depends the whole Law, and also the prophets"

---

[84] Jerome, Ep 52.5; PL 22:531.

[Matt 22:37-40; Luke 10:27]. Therefore blessed Gregory says: "The Lord's precepts are many and they are one: many by reason of the different ways of carrying them out, one by their being rooted in love."[85] If the whole Law and the Prophets depend on these two precepts, and if there is a single benefit to all the commandments, and if it is evident that all the commandments are one, then we do not have to treat all God's commandments individually in this chapter.

But let us see what we have been commanded to do: "You shall love the Lord your God with all your heart." What does it mean to love God with all one's heart? Doesn't it mean that our heart should not tend toward any other love more than to the love of God? For example, if with all our desire we love gold or silver or various possessions and temporal honors or property or animals and other things of this sort, then we do not love God with all our heart. However much the love of our heart is taken up with things like that, that is how much less of our heart there is for God, and that is how much less we love God. Just as a chaste woman who loves her husband loves no other man, so too a person who loves God does not love the world. If we were to love the world, we would not be loving God with our whole heart. And so, let us turn our heart and our mind and all our actions back from loving visible things, and let us love God with our whole heart and our whole soul and our whole strength.

We will be loving God if all the senses that pertain to our mind are free to focus on God,[86] that is, if our intellect serves God, if our wisdom is about God, if our every thought deals with the things that are of God. We will truly be loving God if we are always thinking and speaking about serving him and are doing our utmost to fulfill his commandments. God wants to be loved, not with words alone, but with a pure heart and with just deeds. He does not demand of us gold or silver or anything of that sort, but if we

---

[85] Gregory the Great, *XL Homiliae in Evangelia*, 2.27.1; PL 76:1205.

[86] *Deo vacant.* The Latin *vacare*, used twelve times in RB, by itself means to be free from tasks, to enjoy leisure time. Used with a dative, it means to be free to devote oneself to something or someone.

do possess these things, he orders us to distribute them to the needy. It is ourselves that he is seeking; it is in us that he desires to rest. The only thing God demands of us is that we love him with our whole heart and keep his commandments and preserve our temples undefiled for him, in order that he may always dwell in us and that we may abide in him. Accordingly, let us draw near to him and be united to him by desiring him.

The Lord says next: "You shall love your neighbor as yourself." The Apostle says: "Whoever loves a neighbor has fulfilled the Law" [Rom 13:8]. Conversely, whoever hates is a murderer. If you love your neighbor as yourself, you do not kill that person or lie to the one you love or render false testimony about your neighbor or covet something that belongs to that person. And in addition, what you do not want someone to do to you, you do not do to the one you love as yourself.

Next the Lord says: "On these two commandments depends the whole Law, and also the Prophets." We have already said above that there is a single benefit to all the commandments, and it is clear that all the commandments are one commandment. They cohere in such a way that one could not exist without the other. We cannot love God unless we love our neighbor, and we cannot truly love our neighbor unless we love God. As we said above, it is impossible to treat all God's commandments in this chapter, but we have mentioned briefly and succinctly the things that can spur us on to love God.

We should realize that we must carefully examine not only the Gospel precepts but also the commandments of the prophets and the apostles and observe them very faithfully and obey them. Therefore, let us devote all our energy to loving God with our whole heart, to examining his commandments and always having them before our mind's eye, and to loving them, not in part, but entirely, in order that we may deserve to reach the blessedness that the king, prophet, and hymn-writer speaks of: "Blessed are they who examine the Lord's testimonies; with all their heart they seek him out" [Ps 118:2]. Let us devote ourselves, my brothers, to loving our neighbors as our very selves, so that, together with them, we may without mishap, deserve to reach and to rejoice in the joys that will last forever.

Chapter 27: A Deplorable Description of Those Who Do Not Observe Christ's Precepts

I intended to devote one more chapter to the precepts of our Lord Jesus Christ, but when I recalled that in these days there is hardly anyone who is strong enough to observe them or who is interested in doing so, I wanted to weep rather than write. We really ought to grieve for the present time, in which we see so many thoroughly disgraceful deeds being heaped up every day. If we wanted to consider them all one by one, we would never be able to restrain our tears. Everything has become so confused; everything is falling apart so much that we never see even a trace of virtue. We observe that in our days the world is full of filth and lust and other kinds of wickedness. And what is the most wretched of all evils, we neither reform ourselves nor give an example of reform to others. No, we are like "whitewashed tombs that on the outside seem lovely to people but inside are full of dead people's bones and all kinds of filth" [Matt 23:27].

There is happening to us what happens to people who either go mad or lose their minds: they utter and even do many foul and dangerous things. They feel no shame or repentance. On the contrary, they seem in their own eyes to be more distinguished and wiser than those who are sane and wise. So it is with us: we do everything that is contrary to health and do not even know what health is. If some little sickness happens to strike our body, we immediately summon physicians and give them money and are very careful to do all the appropriate things, and we don't stop until what was bothering us has gotten better. But every day our soul is wounded, lacerated, burned, thrown down, and destroyed in every way, and we don't worry about it at all. But one thing is certain: this lack of care is corrupting and ruining each and every one of us, and all the while there is no one to offer us what will help us and forbid what will harm us. Even though we are all in need of care, there is no one to furnish the medicine of preaching and prescribe the penitence that will cure us. If some religious person from outside our region were to arrive here and see the disarray of Christ's precepts and of our way of living the monastic life, would that person judge anyone else to be greater enemies and antagonists of Christ's precepts than us, and would that person not judge that we had made every effort to act in all matters contrary to what Christ has commanded us?

So that no one may think that I am exaggerating when I say these things, I now cite proofs, not from just anywhere, but from the very commandments of Christ: "You have heard that it was said to people of old: You shall not kill; the one who kills will be liable to judgment. But I say to you, that if you get angry with your brother or sister, you will be liable to judgment, and if you say to your brother or sister: Racha, you will be liable to the council, and if you say: Fool, you will be liable to the Gehenna of fire" [Matt 5:21-22]. These are the words of the Lord Jesus. But we, like unbelieving, faithless people, trample down this Law, and every day we inflict innumerable injuries on our brothers and sisters, as though we hoped to get some reward for doing so.

But let us now see how much difference there is between the justice of the Pharisees and that of Christians. Killing someone makes them liable to judgment, whereas anger makes us likewise liable to judgment. And if anger makes us liable to judgment, how do we dare every day to get angry so easily not only against our juniors but even against our peers and those older than we? As our Lord himself says, we will have to give an account, not only for anger, but for every idle word [see Matt 12:36]. "Racha" means empty and foolish. Since our brothers and sisters believe in Christ even as we do, how do we dare call them empty or foolish or crazy? The fact that the Lord said "racha" and "fool" shows that not even the slightest abuse that we heap on a brother or sister will be overlooked. Hence, we must be convinced that we will be judged for everything, unless we make up for the harm done and do suitable penance in this life. Thus, Christ gave us the judgment that applies to these easy commandments so that we might think the same way about all the others that we transgress.

Furthermore, we put the fear of human beings before the fear of God. If people stronger or more powerful than we injure or insult us, we willingly put up with it without complaint, but even though we have suffered no harm, we often get angry at our equals or inferiors. Who is immune from this fault or a stranger to it? But if an earthly soldier does not dare get angry in the sight of the king and does not dare show any sign of his resentment before the king's eyes, how do we dare get angry in the presence of the eternal King and show our resentment before his face? An earthly king sees the bodies of human beings from the outside, and it is only these bodies that he has in his power, whereas the heavenly King sees into the secret places of our heart and has the power to destroy both of them, body and soul, in Gehenna [see Matt 10:28]. Consequently, we must not neglect this precept, even as regards servants, and we should not get angry at them for no reason, since Christ has bestowed freedom on them just as he has on us. And if we see someone transgressing a commandment of the Lord, we should not get angry at that person. Rather, we ought to have sympathy and compassion, as did the one who said: "Who gets sick, and I do not get sick?" [2 Cor 11:29]. As for what is contained in these next words, who does not take it to be some fable of unbelievers, even though it has been decreed by the eternal voice of God? He says: "If however you are offering your gift at the altar and there remember that your brother or sister has something against you, leave your gift there in front of the altar, and first go and be reconciled with your brother or sister, and then come and offer your gift" [Matt 5:23-24]. And what do we do? As we come to God's altar, we are fighting with each other and are hatching plots in our heart. We do this, even though our God and Lord is so concerned that we be reconciled that he allows his gifts to be left, allows imperfect things to remain in front of the altar, and allows his Mysteries to be interrupted, until we go and get rid of angry feelings and contention and animosity toward our brothers and sisters.

Yet we are not ashamed about this. No, we harbor animosity for days on end and drag out our anger and bad will like a long rope, ignoring the fact that our punishment will last as long as the discord does. What makes our disorder even worse is that, if somebody tells us something good about our enemy, we do not believe it, but if someone says something bad, that we do believe and corroborate it.

If it does happen that we get angry, the Lord orders us to stop being angry before sunset; he says: "Let not the sun set on your feelings of anger" [Eph 4:26]. But we, on the contrary, are not content to drag out our feelings of anger past sunset. We set traps for each other and hope to trip up our neighbors, either by word or by deed. At the time when the sacred gifts are being offered, we have the custom of offering each other the kiss of peace, but I fear that many of us do this only with our lips, even though Christ desires peace not from the mouth but from the heart. That is why we must believe that God is infuriated rather than pleased by these things. Purity and truth are what is pleasing in God's sight, but he detests and hates everything that is pretended and feigned. For every one of these things, we should shed tears and be covered with confusion. In the interest of brevity, we leave the remaining precepts to be discussed concisely and thoroughly in the following chapter.

Chapter 28: Continuing the Same Lamentation as Above

Indeed what is commanded about giving in to the adversary and about forbidden desires, about the right eye, about the right hand and leaving one's wife—we show such contempt for these precepts that it is as though they had never been written or heard [see Matt 5:29-48]. By "right eye" and "right hand" we understand our relatives and associates; that is to say, if they get in the way of our contemplating the true light, we should amputate such bodily members, so that in our efforts to win others we ourselves might not perish for eternity.

I am ashamed to bring up the topic of swearing oaths, not only because of the oaths but also because of perjury [see Matt 5:33-37]. If indeed swearing an oath is a sin and a transgression of a commandment, then what are we to say about perjury? Gospel truth does not allow an oath, even though every word is found to be trustworthy by means of the swearing of an oath [see Matt 18:16; Heb 6:17]. But after these words, the Lord says: "If anyone strikes you on the right cheek, offer that person your other, too, and to the one who wants to take you to court to take away your tunic, surrender your cloak, too. And if anyone forces you to go one mile, go with that person the second mile. Give to the one who asks, and do not turn away from the one who wants to borrow from you" [Matt 5:39-42]. What shall we say to these words? For every one of them, all we can do is shed tears and be covered with confusion, since we openly belong to the camp that opposes them all. We are unwilling to suffer or endure, either in words or in deeds, any of these things that are written. If we are struck in some matter, even if it is only once or lightly, we immediately rise up like wild beasts against those who did it.

Furthermore, even though it is clear that in every situation we act contrary to what Christ commands us, still we learn from him an even nobler way of acting. He says, if someone steals what is yours or hurts or injures you, not only must you not feel resentment because of what he takes from you, but you must love him and with all charity hold yourself in check and even ceaselessly pour out prayers to God for him. It is as though Christ said: Although the person who was out to steal what was yours is fired up by a wicked spirit, if he finds that you are more eager in giving than he had intended to be in stealing, even though he were a savage or barbarian, still he will be ashamed at your goodness. He will be tamed and leave his fury, immediately come to his senses and repent of what he was doing and shudder at his sin, even as he admires and loves the virtue evident in your person.[87]

But where will I find such conduct nowadays? Who lives such a life that I can admire? I do not expect to find anyone who wants patiently to bear this sort of injury. Christ commanded us to pray for those who persecute and slander us, but we set out our spiteful traps, not only for our enemies, but often even for our friends. Christ commanded us to bless those who curse us, but not only do we pay people back in curses many times over, but, if we can, we wound those people with blows in return for their words.

Does it not seem to you, O mortal, that, as I have said, the things we do are completely contrary to Christ's precepts? Don't we fight his commandments rather than obey them? And so, we do well to bemoan and deplore our disobedience. But someone says: Christ commands us to do what is impossible. What are you doing, O mortal? Don't you know how David acted toward Saul [see

---

[87] *tui vero animi virtutem.* As elsewhere, *animus* here refers to the whole person.

1 Sam 24 and 26]? What Stephen the martyr did, who prayed for those who were stoning him [see Acts 7:60]? Are you forgetting what Christ himself taught and did when he said: "Father, forgive them, for they do not know what they are doing" [Luke 23:34]? For those who want to observe Christ's precepts, they are not impossible but easy, whereas for those who do not want to observe them and who disobey them, they seem hard and impossible, even though the Lord says: "My burden is light, and my yoke is pleasant" [Matt 11:30].

Further, what am I to say about what is written in the Lord's prayer: "Forgive us our debts as we forgive our debtors" [Matt 6:12]? Who among us all would dare speak these words to God with confidence? Even if we do nothing to our enemies and debtors, still we keep within us, stored up in our heart, the wound of anger. And even if you do not injure the one who injures you, nevertheless you turn away and do not like to look at that person. Undoubtedly the wound remains in your breast, and the pain increases in your heart. Is that the kind of good will you want God to show to you: that God not injure you but turn away from you and keep your sins in mind and not want to look at you? Therefore, however you want God to be toward you when you are begging pardon for your sins, that is how you should show yourself toward those who have done you wrong, as one of the wise has said: "One person treats another with anger and seeks healing from God" [Sir 28:3]. And if people are not merciful toward each other, how will they gain atonement for their sins?

At this point, I would like to be silent and here put an end to my words, because I am too embarrassed and humiliated to go any further. But what good is being silent, since we are also silently indicted by the very commandments of Christ that we oppose? How can we hide, since the One who knows our hearts will judge them? What, therefore, am I to say about the commandment that orders us not to store up treasure on earth? Some people hear the precept backwards, as it were. It's as though it were said to them: Store up all kinds of treasure on earth. And so they abandon heaven and hold fast to earth; they are crazy about amassing money; with all their heart they hate God but love mammon. As for that saying: "Do not think about tomorrow" [Matt 6:34], I know of no one who hears it, and certainly no one who observes it. That is why I am embarrassed to say anything about this commandment.

When Christ speaks and utters his words, it is incumbent upon us by a kind of pact not to doubt but to believe. But even though in this passage Christ provides the grounds and reasons for his commandments and backs them up with the most apt examples, we are not embarrassed. The reason he uses metaphors of birds that do not plough or sow and lilies that do not spin is so that no one will have any doubt. Yet like the nations, or even perhaps somewhat more hopeless than the nations, we are consumed with thinking about earthly things. About this commandment, as I have said, I am embarrassed to say much. I move on to the next matter. It may be that elsewhere I will find some relief for my shame.

What, therefore, follows these words? "Do not judge, so that you may not be judged" [Matt 7:1]. I thought I would find relief for my shame, but instead I found my humiliation increased. If we were charged with no other sin, this one alone would more than suffice to send us to Gehenna. Indeed, in cases involving the faults of others, we sit as severe and very harsh judges, but we do not see the timbers embedded in our own eyes [see Matt 7:3-5]. You will find hardly anyone free from this sin, neither a person of the world nor a monk nor even a solitary. We are not even terrified at what the Lord also says: "With the judgment you use to judge you will be judged" [Matt 7:2]. Now tell me, how much effort does it take to keep from judging someone else? But even though we can effortlessly obey God's commandment, we labor and exert ourselves in order to transgress it. Indeed our Lord declared about his commandments that there is nothing burdensome in them, as I related a little earlier: "My yoke is pleasant and my burden is light" [Matt 11:30]. But we have turned things around and made heavy what he established as light. Although there may be some things that demand a little labor, nevertheless whatever he has commanded is light, even if it be a hardship. And if it is a hardship, how can it be light? It is light, I say, because the immense weight of future glory makes the hardship of the present time light [see 2 Cor 4:17].

Next it says: "Do not give what is holy to dogs nor cast your pearls in front of pigs" [Matt 7:6]. Corrupted as we are by the love of praise and the vice of boasting, we turn this precept around, too.

We exercise no discretion and lay bare the secrets of mysteries to people who don't have pure understanding, to people who don't hold onto a healthy faith, and, even worse, to people who are implicated in the filthy deeds of sinners.

It would be an immense undertaking to discuss every single commandment that people hold in contempt in various ways, like this one: "Whatever you want people to do to you, do that to them" [Matt 7:12]. But we do just the opposite: we do everything to people that we do not want to suffer. Likewise, we who are commanded to walk along on the narrow road are always walking on the wide one [see Matt 7:13-14]. The very people who seem to have taken up their cross and followed Christ take great pains to discover the wide and spacious road. How do those people act who are getting ready to leave the world behind? When they are making careful inquiry about monasteries or places of reclusion or about the places where they might live, they inquire above all about quiet and convenience. Their very first concern and their first words are these: Is it quiet in the place that I am to go to? Will I be able to get there plenty of everything I need? The first thing, as I have said, that they are careful to ask about is, whether any of those things are missing that the wide and spacious road demands. What are you doing, O mortal? What are you saying? You have been commanded to walk the narrow and cramped road, so why are you inquiring about quiet and plenty?

Perhaps someone may think that in saying these things I am just finding fault, so I will now tell my own story. At the time when I began to think of renouncing the world and taking up a life in solitude, I know how carefully I thought over within my mind where I would live and how, in my solitude, I would be provided with those things that I would need for the body. I was not slack in inquiring where I would get clothing and lights, where I would get wood and vegetables and things like that. I was thinking over and over in detail about how to provide rest for the body. Alas, how subtly does that craftsman of evil, the devil, deceive us, and with what total blindness does he cover the eyes of our mind! We want to ascend to the kingdom of heaven, and we are inquiring whether we will meet any difficulties on the road. We are hastening to the peak and the riches of heaven, to those riches, I say, that "eye has not seen nor ear heard nor the human heart conceived" [1 Cor 2:9], and yet we are making careful inquiry about rest for the body.

As I said above, it would be an immense undertaking to discuss each one of Christ's commandments in this place. Nonetheless, it is up to us to weep and lament for every one of these commandments that we violate and despise, so that with God's help we may, by the copious floods of our tears, deserve to be washed and purified from the sins that we have committed by disobeying and despising those same commandments of Christ.

Chapter 29: Compunction of Heart

Compunction of heart is humility of mind, with tears and remembrance of sins and fear of judgment. From the virtue of humility is born compunction of heart; from compunction of heart is begotten repentance, and from repentance is gained forgiveness of sins.

There are four kinds of sentiment by which the mind of a just person experiences compunction and a healthy loathing. They are: remembering past sins, recalling punishments to come, considering how one is on pilgrimage in the misery of this present life, and desiring to reach our native land on high and to be able to get there as soon as possible. When these four are in the heart, then one may believe that God is present in the human heart by grace.

In addition, if our desire for compunction of heart is to be perfect, it is incumbent upon us first to have withdrawn both mind and heart from every disturbance and fluctuation caused by visible things and to have mounted up to that silence where there is the utmost quiet, unbroken tranquility, and pure serenity. It is on that point that we should focus all our attention and always keep our mind's eye fixed. We ought to keep before the eyes of our mind the day of death and call our past sins to mind. We should recall those who groan in hell and what it is like for the souls that are there, in what bitter silence they are, in what despairing lamentation, what fear, what torture, what dread and pain. On their account we ought to shed infinite tears. But let us reflect upon the day of resurrection and upon that terrifying, dreadful, and fearful judgment of Christ, and upon the reward given to the just and the punishment awaiting sinners that they will suffer in God's sight. Let us call to mind all the tortures, the inextinguishable fire, the worm that does not die, and the pit of darkness [see Mark 9:43-44]. And above all, let us dread the gnashing of teeth and unending torments. Let us also set before ourselves the good things and joyous gladness that are awaiting the just in the presence of God and his angels in eternal glory. Let us also ponder how glorious are those choirs of angels, the fellowship that blessed spirits enjoy, and how majestic is the vision of God. Let us keep the memory of both these things always in our hearts: let us grieve over the judgment pronounced on sinners, but let us rejoice over the good things that await the just. If we do, then the perfect compunction that springs from fear will hand the soul over to the compunction that springs from love.[88]

Chapter 30: The Two Kinds of Compunction

There are two kinds of compunction, that is, the kind that is watered from above and the kind that is watered from below. You receive the kind watered from below when in your weeping you dread the tortures of hell. You receive the kind watered from above when you afflict yourself with tears because you desire the heavenly kingdom. It should be kept in mind that the person who has been given to immoderate laughing and joking will not be able to reach compunction of heart. People who are endeavoring to ascend to perfection should have no part in joking like silly children or in bursting out with laughter through dissolute lips. Rather they should show their happiness of mind simply by smiling. Laughing loudly is insanity. Playing is for children; mourning is for the perfect. Joking and laughter make a just person careless and lukewarm in serving God.

O how much harm laughing and joking do! Conversely how much benefit do weeping and mourning bring! The person who likes to laugh now will afterward weep very bitterly, whereas the person who willingly mourns now will afterward rejoice endlessly.

---

[88] See RB 7.67.

Indeed our Savior called blessed those who mourn, and he says that those who are happy now will weep on the last day [see Luke 6:21, 25]. The apostle James says: "Be heartsick and mourn; let your laughter be turned into mourning and your joy into grief" [Jas 4:9]. Solomon has this to say: "Laughter will be mixed with sorrow" [Prov 14:13]. And Gregory declares: "No one can both rejoice here with the world and reign there with Christ."[89] In addition, we read in the conferences of the fathers: "An elder saw someone laughing and said to him: 'In the presence of heaven and earth we are to give an account for our whole life, and you are laughing?'"[90] Accordingly we should not take delight in childish joking and laughing but in sacred reading and singing spiritual melodies. Our hearts may well be too hard to produce tears, but as soon as the sweet music of the psalms begins to sound, our spirit becomes attuned to compunction of heart. There are many people who are so moved by the sweet music of chant that they bewail their sins, and they are all the more attuned to producing tears by the influence of the gentle sweetness that resounds in the voice singing the psalms.

Yet we must try to preserve within us the vigor of tears, even when the times of compunction have passed, insofar as we can by God's grace. Otherwise, after we have experienced compunction of heart, our flowing thought will dissolve us, empty happiness will steal away our mind, and our soul will lose, by the careless flow of thought, the profit it gained from compunction of heart.

Why does the soul deserve to obtain what it had asked for? Because after tears it kept itself in the same lively state of mind. It is no surprise, then, that it is written: "Her face was no longer changed toward diverse things" [1 Sam 1:18]. Because she did not forget what she was asking for, she was not deprived of the favor that she pleaded for. But we, who after baptism have defiled our life, should rebaptize our conscience with tears. Therefore if we pour out tears unceasingly but nonetheless do not stop sinning, we have the lamenting but not the cleansing. But where tears are flowing in abundance, there filthy thoughts do not come near. Compunction

---

[89] Gregory the Great, *XL Homiliae in Evangelia*, 1.12.4; PL 76:1117.
[90] *Vitae patrum*, 5.3.23; PL 73:864.

is health of soul; compunction is illumination of mind; compunction is forgiveness of sins; compunction makes the Holy Spirit dwell in us.

Chapter 31: Concerning Reverence and Persistence in Prayer

We must know beyond any doubt and truly believe that by perseverance in prayer we can obtain forgiveness for all our sins, so long as our actions do not contradict our prayer or our lips belie what is in our heart.[91] It is better to pray with the heart silently and without the sound of the voice than to pray only with words without a focused mind. After all, God does not attend to begging words but looks upon a heart that prays. Indeed careless prayers cannot obtain what they want even from a human being. If we want to put requests before powerful people, we do not presume to do so, except with humility and respect. All the more reason, then, to entreat the Lord God of all things with humility of heart and pure devotion. And we should realize that we will be heard, not because of much talk but because of purity of heart. Consequently, prayer ought to be short and pure, unless perhaps it be prolonged by a desire inspired by God's grace.[92]

Therefore, when we stand to pray, we should sigh and weep. We should recall how serious are the sins we have committed and how painful the punishments of hell that we fear. That soul is surely far from God which, during prayer, is absorbed in thoughts of the world. Only then are we really praying when our thoughts are not somewhere else. But rare indeed are the people who make such prayers, and even if some people do, nevertheless it is difficult for them always to pray like that. The devil does his best to suggest thoughts about worldly affairs to our minds precisely when he catches sight of us praying. Conversely, we ought to persevere and not give up praying until we overcome the distracting thoughts about worldly matters that the enemy has secretly introduced into our minds. As often as you are affected by some vice, that is how

---

[91] See RB 19.7.
[92] The foregoing four sentences reproduce with few changes RB 20.1-4.

often you should apply yourself to prayer, because frequent prayer crushes the attack of the vices. And if you are wounded, you should not stop praying for those who wound you, because just as medicine does a wound no good if the blade is still in it, so too prayer does you no good if you still keep the pain in your mind and harbor hatred in your heart.

When we pray, our desire for God should be so strong that we do not give up hope that our prayer will be answered. Our prayer is empty if we do not have confident hope. The Apostle tells us: "Let each person ask in faith and not waver. For the one who doubts is like an ocean wave that is moved by the wind and is dispersed" [Jas 1:6]. Our uncertainty arises from the fact that we still sense that we are attached to a desire to sin. The Apostle says: "The persevering petition of a just person is very powerful" [Jas 5:16]. The reason prayer is powerful is that by it the demons are overcome and are prevented from entering and going around wherever they want. In the Tripartite History we read:

> In the days of Julian the Apostate, a demon was sent by him into the West to go quickly and bring back to him from there a certain answer. But when the demon had arrived in a certain place where a certain monk was living, he stood still on the spot for ten days; he could go no further because the monk did not cease praying either night or day. The demon went back to the one who had sent him without having accomplished his task. Upon his return, Julian said to him: What took you so long? The demon said in answer: I was delayed and have come back without having done my work. I waited ten days for the monk Publius, to see whether he would stop praying and I could move on, but he didn't stop, and I was prevented from moving on and have come back without having done the work. Then the most sacrilegious Julian became indignant and said: When I go there, I'll revenge myself on him. A few days later, by God's providence, Julian died. Immediately one of the prefects who was in his service went and sold everything he had and came to that elder and became a great monk. He stayed with him until he fell asleep in the Lord.[93]

---

[93] *Vitae patrum*, 6.2.12; PL 73:1003.

By this account we are given to understand that the constant prayer of God's servants not only saves human beings but even vanquishes the darts of the devil. By means of very pure prayers, God bestows on us everything that we need and beyond doubt puts to flight everything that is harmful. Consequently we have to pray without interruption with mouth and heart.

Chapter 32: How Someone Can Pray Without Ceasing

A servant of God, especially a solitary, is obliged to pray, to read, and to work without interruption. Otherwise a malevolent spirit may invade the mind that is idle. For it is by prayers that we are cleansed, by reading that we are instructed, and by toil that we tire out the body by work, so that it does not become proud.

Now we must inquire how it is possible for someone to pray without interruption. Some people want to say that a person who observes the canonical hours is praying without interruption. But we should not stop praying during the other hours. Rather, as the Apostle says, we ought to pray without interruption [see 1 Thess 5:17]. We will be able to fulfill this precept with the Lord's mercy, that is to say, if we cannot constantly be praying with our tongue, then we should pray with our heart, and if we are unable to pray ceaselessly with either our mouth or our heart, then our actions should be such that they will always pray to God on our behalf.

We are given an example of this in the conferences of the fathers.

> Abba Lucius questioned some brothers and said: What manual work do you do? They said in response: We do not touch any manual work, but, as the Apostle says, we pray without inter-ruption. The elder said to them: Don't you eat? They said: Yes, we do. And he said to them: So when you are eating, who is praying for you? And he posed them a second question: Don't you sleep? They said: Yes, we do. And the elder went on: When you are sleeping, who is praying for you? They could come up with no answer. He continued: Pardon me, brothers, but you are not doing what you said. Now I will show you how, by working with my hands, I pray without interruption. I sit down, and, with God's help, I soak a few

palm leaves and make a woven mat and say: "Have mercy on me, O God, according to your great compassion, and according to the multitude of your mercies erase my iniquity" [Ps 50:1]. And he said to them: This is prayer, isn't it? They said to him: Yes. But he said: When I keep working all day and praying with mouth or heart, I earn six coins, more or less. Two of them I give to the poor outside the gate, and the rest I spend for my needs and those of my disciples. But the one who took those two denarii prays on my behalf while I am eating or sleeping. This is the way that, by God's grace, what is written is fulfilled in me: "Pray without interruption" [1 Thess 5:17].[94]

That is why, as has been said, we must ceaselessly pray with mouth or heart, or do the kind of work that will pray to God on our behalf.

What the Lord said, however, seems to contradict this command of the Apostle: "When you pray, do not speak much, as the Gentiles do" [Matt 6:7]. But notice that the Lord did not say: Do not pray much, but rather: Do not speak much, as the Gentiles do, who pray with the polished wordiness of facile eloquence. Do you want to pray to God without interruption? Then forgive a brother or sister who sins against you; seek praise, not from human beings, but from God; close the door of your heart's chamber in the face of the crowd of empty fantasies, and keep your prayer from being blocked in any way by fixing your mind's eye on the love of God.

Chapter 33: All Empty Thoughts Are Illusions Worked by Demons

In the manner of life lived by God's servants,[95] there is no virtue that demands so much labor as does prayer. When people wish to pray to their God, the demons always hasten to interrupt their prayer, because they know that no other activity so thwarts them as does prayer poured out to God. Indeed, even though people who are living according to a religious manner of life[96] perform

---

[94] Vitae patrum, 5.12.9; PL 73:942.
[95] in conversatione servorum dei
[96] in conversatione religiosa

every other labor incessantly, still they do have some rest. But prayer,
as has been said, has no rest.

Concerning this we read in the lives of the fathers:

> Once, a demon knocked during the night at the door of the
> cell of blessed Macarius and said: Get up, Abba Macarius, and
> let us go to the assembly where the brothers are gathering for
> vigils. But he, who by God's grace was filled with prudence,
> could not be deceived. He realized that it was a trick of the
> devil and said: O you liar and enemy of truth, what do you
> have to do with the assembly and congregation of the holy
> ones? But the demon said: Is it hidden from you, O Macarius,
> that no congregation of monks does anything without us?
> Macarius said: May the Lord command you, you unclean one.
> But the demon went on: Just come, and you will see our works.
> Having said these words, the demon departed. The abba went
> back to his prayer and asked God to show him if what the
> demon had boasted about were true. And so he went to the
> assembly where vigils were being celebrated by the brothers.
> Again he pleaded with the Lord in prayer to show him the
> truth of the matter. Suddenly he saw throughout the whole
> church creatures like little Ethiopian boys running this way
> and that and flying around. The little Ethiopian boys that were
> running around were playing with each of those who were
> sitting there. If they pressed on someone's eyes with two
> fingers, that person immediately fell asleep. If they put a finger
> in his mouth, they made him yawn. When the brothers pros-
> trated themselves to pray after a psalm, the creatures kept right
> on running around, and in front of one brother prostrate in
> prayer they turned into what looked like a woman. In front
> of another they appeared like people building something or
> carrying something or doing various things. Whatever the
> demons acted out in their play, that was what those praying
> were pondering in their heart. But when they began to do
> these sorts of things in front of some of the brothers, they were
> given something like a push and were knocked over and
> thrown down, and so they didn't dare stand in front of them
> anymore or even pass near them. They were even playing on
> the backs and necks of other brothers. When the holy Macarius
> saw these things, he groaned deeply and said with tears: Arise,

O Lord, that your enemies may be dispersed and flee from your face [see Ps 67:2], since our soul is filled with illusions [see Ps 122:4]. When the prayer was over, he called to him each of the brothers in front of whom the demons had been playing with their different illusions. He asked each one to tell him whether, during prayer, he had been thinking about building or carrying or doing the various things for which he had seen the demons making images for each brother. Each one of them confessed that it had been in their heart, just as he accused them. Then it was understood that all the useless and superfluous thoughts that each person conceives during the time of sleep or psalmody or prayer are illusions that come from the demons. But from those who kept careful guard over their heart, the Ethiopians were easily repulsed. The mind that is joined to God and that is focused on him, especially during the time of prayer, takes in nothing foreign, nothing superfluous.[97]

Chapter 34: God and the Angels Are Always Present to Those Who Are Singing and Chanting Psalms[98]

Although we know that God is everywhere by the power of his divinity, and although we believe that his eyes watch the good and the bad, we believe beyond a shadow of a doubt that he is especially present to us when we participate in the Divine Office. Thus we are always mindful of what the prophet says: "Serve the Lord in fear" [Ps 2:11], and: "Sing psalms wisely" [Ps 46:8]. We should believe that the angelic spirits are most present to us when we are discharging the duties we owe to God, that is, when we attune our ear to the sacred readings or give our attention to psalmody or devote ourselves to prayer or celebrate the solemn rites of the Mass. That is why the prophet says: "In the sight of the angels I will sing psalms to you" [Ps 137:1]. Consequently, when we have assembled for the Divine Office or to celebrate the solemn rites of the Mass, we should devote all our skill and energy to keeping constantly in mind how we ought to be in the sight of

---

[97] *Vitae patrum*, 3.43; PL 73:765.
[98] The first half of this chapter depends heavily on RB 19.

God and of his angels. And let us stand to sing the psalms in such a way that our mind is in harmony with our voice, as the Apostle says: "I will sing psalms with my spirit; I will also sing psalms with my mind" [1 Cor 14:15].

We must, however, be careful not to celebrate the Divine Office negligently or halfheartedly or disgracefully, and we must not be lazy and arrive late. If we do—may it never happen—then we will come under the condemnation that says: Cursed be the person who does the work of God negligently [see Deut 27:15]. We must be very careful not to commit anything shameful or indecent or improper or perverse in either our thoughts or words or actions. Rather, we should perform our heavenly duty with fear and reverence, since we have been made worthy to stand in the presence of God and of his angels. Then the Lord, when he comes to us, will find in us nothing to condemn but rather something to reward.

Chapter 35: The Praise of the Psalms and the Arrangement of the Hours at Which We Ought to Sing Psalms

Unflagging chanting of the psalms consoles sad hearts, makes minds more well-disposed, delights those who feel disgust, puts new life into the lifeless, and invites sinners to lament. Even though our hearts are hard, nevertheless, as soon as the sweetness of the psalms begins sounding, it attunes our whole self [99] to make progress in piety. The sweetness of the psalms softens all hardness of heart, and just as we are guided by the prayers we say, so let us take delight in devoting ourselves to the psalms. Only in this life do we pour out prayer as a remedy for sins, but the chanting of psalms represents the perpetual praise of God and everlasting glory. And so it is written: "Blessed are they who dwell in your house, O Lord; for ages of ages they will praise you" [Ps 83:5]. Those who carry out the regularity of this work faithfully and with attentive mind

---

[99] *Animus*, here juxtaposed to *dura corda*, "hard hearts," signifies the whole of the person's understanding, will, disposition, and temper.

become, as it were, companions of the angels. For this reason we need to perform the offices that our service involves at set hours and times, namely, morning office,[100] Prime, Terce, Sext, None, Vespers, and Compline. About these daytime hours the prophet David says: "Seven times during the day have I spoken praise to you" [Ps 118:164], but about the nighttime Vigils the same prophet says: "At midnight I arose to confess to you" [Ps 118:62].[101] And he also says: "At night I remembered your name, O Lord" [Ps 118:55], and he also says: "If I remembered you on my bed, in early morning" [Ps 62:7].

Consequently, at times other than the Divine Offices at night and the other hours during the day, we should not leave off praying, but throughout the intervals between the hours, let us always be either praying or reading or doing some manual work and so keep our heart and thoughts from becoming bored. This is just what we read blessed Anthony did.

> Once he was sitting in the wilderness, and his mind[102] was encountering thoughts of boredom and confusion because he was at that time not yet laboring continually. He said to God: O Lord, I want to be saved, but my thoughts won't let me. What shall I do in this predicament and how shall I be saved? After a short time he got up and went outside, and he saw someone that looked like him sitting there and working. Finally he saw the person stand up from work and pray and then sit back down and make a mat out of palm leaves and then again stand up to pray. Now it was an angel of the Lord who had been sent to correct and advise Anthony. After seeing these things, he heard the voice of the angel, who said: Do this and you will be saved. When he had heard this, he was filled with joy and confidence. And by acting in this way from then on, he found the salvation that he sought.[103]

---

[100] *matutino*, i.e., the morning office (Lauds) as distinct from the night office.

[101] The foregoing three sentences depend on RB 16.1-5.

[102] *Animus* is here joined with *cogitationes*, "thoughts," and is best rendered "mind," though it regularly refers to the whole of a person's inner life.

[103] *Vitae patrum*, 5.7.1; PL 73:893.

We too, with God's help, will be saved by acting in this way.

We have made no attempt to spell out the number and length of the psalms that we ought to chant each day. Far be it from me to set limits to what the Apostle commands us to do without interruption. Let the conscience of each one bear witness, because each of us at every hour has God as the Searcher of our heart, from whom nothing lies hidden [see Rom 8:27; 1 Chr 28:9]. We are also bound to pray unceasingly for our benefactors and for all people, for kings and all those in high positions, so that we may be able to lead quiet and tranquil lives [see 1 Tim 2:2]. Furthermore, we should know for certain that, the more persistent we are in praying, the more joyous the reward we will receive in eternal bliss.

Solitaries must be conscientious in providing their oratories during the night with lights either that they have made themselves or that the faithful have given as offerings.

Chapter 36: Whether Anyone Should Dare to Receive the Body of the Lord or to Chant Mass Every Day

I do not rely on my own opinion but on the judgment of the holy fathers when I say that I believe both of these may be done, that is, to celebrate Mass every day and to receive every day with fear and trembling the most holy Mysteries of the Lord's Body and Blood. But only those may do so who are clean of any defilement of flesh or spirit and who do so with great awe and dread, because those who desire to receive such a Guest within them must be not only chaste in body but also clean of heart. There once was a venerable father by the name of Apollonius, who

> used to advise the brothers that, if possible, they receive in Communion the Mysteries of Christ every day, for fear that those who distanced themselves from them would be distancing themselves from God. He said that people who receive Communion frequently without any doubt are frequently receiving the Savior himself, because he himself says: "Whoever eats my flesh and drinks my blood remains in me and I in him" [John 6:57]. Since this commemoration of the Lord's passion is to be celebrated conscientiously by God's servants,

the first thing that they must keep in mind is that each one make every effort to be found prepared and not be judged unworthy of the Lord's Mysteries.[104]

On this last matter, blessed Gregory says in the Book of Dialogues: "We ought to despise the present age with our whole mind, to offer to God daily sacrifices of tears, and to immolate the daily oblations of his Body and Blood. It is these sacrificial victims especially that save the soul from eternal ruin."[105] But when we offer these sacrifices, we must immolate ourselves by the contrition of our heart. I say this confidently: if we ourselves are oblations for God before our death, then after our death we will not be lacking the oblations that will save us. That is why is it good that, whatever we hope others will do for us after our death, we ourselves do that thing while we are alive. It is more blessed to go out from prison a free person than, after one's chains are gone, still to be seeking freedom.

In the same book, the pope continues speaking on this subject:

> There was a man of venerable life, Cassius, bishop of Narnia, whose custom it was to offer daily sacrifice to God. Hardly a day went by when he did not immolate a sacrifice of propitiation to God. While he was immolating himself by his tears, he received a command of the Lord through a vision experienced by one of his priests: Do what you are doing; perform what you are performing. Let not your foot stop; let not your hand cease. On the birthday of the apostles, you will come to me, and I will give you your reward. Seven years later, as he was celebrating the solemnity of the Mass on the very birthday of the apostles and had received the Mysteries of Holy Communion, he went forth from the body.[106]

This event makes us realize what a protection it is to immolate every day the sacrificial victims of the most holy Body and Blood

---

[104] Rufinus, *Historia monachorum*, 7 "*de Apollonio*"; PL 21:418–19
[105] Gregory the Great, *Dialogorum libri*, 4.58; PL 77:425.
[106] Ibid., 4.56; PL 77:424.

of our Lord Jesus Christ. It is manifestly clear how health-giving
it is to be given such a medicine. That is why a certain venerable
poet said:

> A great protection it is to be fed on the sacred libation,
> if no sins weigh down the heart of the participant.[107]

And on this same topic, the eminent doctor Augustine said: "A
Christian ought to fear nothing more than to be separated from
the Body of Christ. For if you are separated from the Body of
Christ, you are not a member of him. If you are not a member of
him, then your spirit is not infused with life. As the Apostle says:
'Whoever does not have Christ's spirit does not belong to him'
[Rom 8:9]."[108]

It follows that we should all consult our faith and then do what
we devoutly believe we should do. We know that those two did
not quarrel between themselves, and neither one put himself before
the other—I am speaking of Zacchaeus and the centurion. The
former joyfully received the Lord, while the latter said: "I am not
worthy, O Lord, that you come under my roof" [Luke 7:6]. Both
of them were honoring the Savior, but in diverse and, as it were,
contrary ways. Both were sorry for their sins, and both were seeking mercy. In the same way, one person honors the Sacrament of
the Lord's Body and Blood and does not dare to receive it daily,
while another likewise honors the Sacrament and does not dare to
omit receiving it for a single day.

Chapter 37: Whether Someone May Celebrate Mass or Not, After the Illusion That Sometimes Happens in Dreams

As blessed Gregory says, "in dealing with the illusion that sometimes happens in a dream, there is great need for discretion in
distinguishing the reason this happened to the mind of the one

---

[107] Prosper of Aquitaine, *Epigrammatum ex Sententiis S. Augustini*, 72; PL 51:520.
[108] Augustine, *In Iohannis Evangelium Tractatus*, 27.6; PL 35:1618.

sleeping. Sometimes it happens because of overindulgence, sometimes because of a natural superfluity or a disease, sometimes because of a thought. When it occurs because of a natural superfluity or a disease, this illusion is not to be feared at all," [109] as the prophet says: "The Lord knows how we are made" [Ps 102:14]. When this happens, he should simply wash with water. Then he may participate in the divine Sacraments.

But when the stomach's craving carries him away and he eats more than he should, with the result that the receptacles of the fluids are overburdened, the person[110] thereby incurs a certain guilt, but not to the extent of preventing him from receiving the Sacraments or of celebrating the solemnities of the Mass, when for example a feast day requires that he do so or he is forced to exercise his ministry, since there is no other priest in the locale, or love of offering the sacrifice compels him to resolve[111] to do so. If there are others present who can fulfill the Mystery,[112] the illusion that happened because of overindulgence should not prevent him from receiving the sacred Mystery, but, in my opinion, he should humbly abstain from immolating the divine Sacrament until he has been reconciled by worthy tears and has washed himself with water and so can approach once again the sacred Mysteries.

If, however, the illusion of the sleeper's mind arises from filthy thoughts he entertained while awake, then his guilt is obvious to himself.[113] He sees from what root the defilement arose, since what he thought while conscious he carried out while unconscious. When this occurs, he must humbly withdraw himself from the divine Mysteries and first wash away with water the filth of the body and cleanse by penance the wound of the heart. Finally, with the Lord's mercy, he may be reconciled to the life-giving Sacraments.

---

[109] Pseudo-Gregory, *Epistula*, 11, Ep 64; PL 77:1198.

[110] *animus*

[111] Again, *animus*.

[112] The Holstenius-Brockie text has *implere mysterium*. Possibly an original *ministerium*, "ministry," was erroneously copied as *mysterium*. The latter word occurs several times in the next few lines.

[113] *animus*

For in the Gospel, the Lord says: "Whoever looks at a woman to desire her, has already committed adultery with her in his heart" [Matt 5:28]. He says "in his heart," not in his body. Likewise the Scripture elsewhere warns us: "Be very careful to protect your heart" [Prov 4:23].

There are some people in whom illusions of this sort frequently arise but whose spirits,[114] even when asleep, are not defiled by filthy imaginings. In such a case, one thing is clear: that the mind itself is not guilty and is, by its own judgment, free from blame, since it does not remember having seen anything while the body was asleep. Indeed, as one of the fathers said, "If something like that happens in sleep without women being imagined, it is not a sin. The large amount of fluid in the body, when it has filled its own receptacles, must be dispersed by way of its channels. But when the sight of women and the enticements of the flesh occur during sleep, if it happens because of useless and seductive thoughts, then it is a sin."[115]

Furthermore, it should be noted that there are three bodily movements. One is natural. The second comes from being full of food, when the body is nourished and warmed by food and drink, which give rise to heat and blood and which excite the body to seek pleasure. On this account, the Lord says: "Watch out that your hearts not be weighed down by over-eating and drunkenness" [Luke 21:34]. The third motion comes from the plotting and envy of demons. That is why we must restrain this very overabundance and flowing of pleasures by great self-control, by many fasts and by continuous prayers. As the blessed Augustine says: "Just as a wounded enemy does not do us any harm, so the mortified flesh does not disturb our soul."[116]

Finally, people who live a life of pleasure, if a sickness of their body should so demand, abstain without delay from all those things that the doctor has deemed harmful. Why then do we not do so

---

[114] *animus*

[115] Source not located.

[116] Defensor of Ligugé, *Liber scintillarum*, 8.5, identified as Augustine; PL 88:632. Original source not located.

all the more, we who should be seeking health of soul and spirit? The Lord ought to have the kind of ministers who are untouched by any corruption of the flesh and who are radiant with chaste self-control in mind and body.

Chapter 38: Constancy in Reading and Prayer

We ought to practice constancy in reading and perseverance in prayer. Constancy in reading fortifies a person against sin, as the prophet says: "In my heart I have hidden your utterances, so that I do not sin against you" [Ps 118:11]. These are the weapons, namely, reading and prayer, that overcome the devil and win eternal blessedness. These are the weapons that subdue the vices and nourish the virtues. In reading and prayer you can look at yourself as in a kind of mirror and see what sort of person you are, where you are heading, and how you are progressing. Consequently, if you want always to be with God, you should read frequently and pray frequently. For when we pray, we are speaking with God, and when we read, God is speaking with us.

Reading the Sacred Scriptures confers on us a twofold gift: first, it forms the mind's understanding, and, second, it draws a person away from the world's vanity and leads toward the love of God. Persevering reading arouses fear of Gehenna, purifies the soul, and incites the heart of the reader to desire the joys of heaven. Just as the flesh is fed by fleshly foods, so the inner person is nourished and sustained on divine utterances, as the prophet says: "How sweet to my throat are your utterances, O Lord, more than honey and honeycomb to my mouth" [Ps 118:103].

It is clear that all Scripture was written in order to save and teach us, so that, by the encouragement we derive from the Scriptures, we may make progress in good actions. Just as a blind person stumbles more often than does someone who can see, so a person who is ignorant of God's law sins more often through ignorance than does one who knows it. Many people are gifted with quick understanding, but they neglect to devote themselves to reading, and what they could have known by reading they do not know through their neglect.

There are many people who read and yet fast from what they read. About them the prophet says: "You sow much and harvest little; you eat and are not satisfied; you drink and are not made drunk" [Hag 1:6]. You sow a great deal in your heart but receive little when you know many things about the heavenly commandments through either reading or hearing but are negligent in putting them into practice and so yield little. You eat and are not satisfied when you hear God's words yet crave the world's wealth or glory. You drink and are not made drunk when you give ear to the voice that is reading or preaching but do not have a change of mind. You have drunk and have not been made drunk when you have desired to acquire the things that belong to this world.

We know that the mind of people who drink becomes confused by drunkenness. People who have become drunk[117] have undoubtedly had a change of mind; they no longer seek earthly things and no longer love the empty and transitory things they used to love. Most blessed of all is the person who reads the divine Scriptures and converts the words into deeds. Now no one can know the meaning of Sacred Scripture fully except by becoming familiar with it by reading. Just as the earth yields a more abundant crop the more thoroughly it is cultivated, so too, the more frequently you read Sacred Scripture, the more abundant will be the understanding you gain from it.

Solitaries should not read the books of the gentiles, for fear that the entertaining and silly fables or the fictions of the poets that are found in them may arouse the mind to crave after wrongful pleasures. Then too, they should not go prying into the secrets of God, as Scripture says: "Do not seek for things too high for you, and do not search into matters too potent for you" [Sir 3:22]. That is why the Apostle adds in awe: "O the depth of the riches of God's knowledge and wisdom! How inscrutable are his judgments, and how unsearchable his ways!" [Rom 11:33].

Consequently we must be very cautious in meditating on the things we read and also very cautious about prying into their meaning. According to the commands of the Apostle, let us hold

---

[117] I.e., on God's word.

fast to what is right and refute what is contrary to the truth. Let us be so instructed in what is good that, with God's help, we will stay unharmed by what is evil.

Chapter 39: The Daily Manual Work of Solitaries

If at times we stop praying and reading, we ought to apply ourselves to working with our hands. That is why it is written: Idleness is the enemy of the soul. When our ancient foe finds someone who is idle, he easily carries that person off into sin. Indeed our holy fathers and the apostles used to live by the labor of their hands.[118] Accordingly the Apostle writes to the Thessalonians: "You yourselves know how you ought to imitate us. For we did not waste our time when we were among you, nor did we eat someone else's bread without paying for it. No, in labor and toil we worked night and day with our hands, so that we would not be a burden to any of you. Not as though we did not have the power to, just as others do, but so that we might offer ourselves as a pattern by which you might imitate us. For when we were still with you, we used to order that, if anyone did not want to work, then that person should not eat" [2 Thess 3:7-10]. Now since this holy apostle who preached the Gospel did not want to eat bread without paying for it, but rather earned his food in labor and toil, what makes us think that we have the right to leave our hands idle and eat bread without paying for it? After all, not only have we not been commissioned to preach the word, but we have not been charged with the care of a single soul but our own.

So then, we have to labor with our hands because it is good to provide for our own livelihood and to have something to give to those who are suffering want. Thus Saint Caesarius said: "You ought to devote yourselves to reading and prayer in such a way that you also put your hands to work on something."[119] Indeed

---

[118] The foregoing relies on RB 48.1, 8.

[119] Defensor, 8.5, identified as Caesarius; PL 88:616; see CC 117:34, where the source is given as *Regul. Monast.* 2.7; Morin 140, 11–12. This saying of Caesarius is found in *Epistola II ad Caesariam abbatissam ejusque congregatione* (PL 67:1132) and in *Epistola Sancti Caesarii ad quosdam germanos* (PL 67:1157).

you should devote the major part of the day to holy work. But we must ask why the Teacher of the Nations, the Preacher of the Gospel, says that he did not eat someone else's bread without paying for it, since he knew that the Lord had ordered that "those who proclaim the Gospel should live from the Gospel" [1 Cor 9:14], and also: Workers are worth their wage and their food [see Luke 10:7; Matt 10:10]. He worked with his hands to earn his livelihood, because it was an unworthy thing to accept anything from those who eagerly pursued error. That person sins and loses the freedom to preach who accepts remuneration from someone who gives to keep from being reprimanded. That is why the Apostle says: "I am permitted to do everything, but not everything is good for me to do" [1 Cor 6:12]. He spoke this way because he was permitted to receive his expenses from those to whom he was preaching, but since he knew that the pseudo-apostles were looking for an excuse to receive their expenses, he did not want to take anything from those people, lest the vitality of gospel truth grow listless on account of the stomach. Indeed, you cannot earnestly censure one from whom you accept payment.

Even though the Apostle, in the situation mentioned above, chose to labor with his hands to earn his livelihood, nevertheless, whenever he needed to, he did accept food from the faithful. Once, when he was enduring great privation, the brethren sent him what he needed to assist him in his privation. He answered and thanked them: "You were kind to share in my privations. I have learned to make do in whatever circumstances I find myself. I know how to be hungry and to have plenty; I have learned how to suffer want. I can do all things in the One who strengthens me. But you were really very kind to send something to take care of my needs" [Phil 4:14, 11-13]. This passage shows that Paul sometimes accepted from the faithful what he needed to sustain himself. Because of this, the blessed Augustine advices us: "Those who cannot support themselves by working with their hands, as Paul did, should accept from the people the sustenance they need, but they should not neglect the infirmity of others."[120] He says: "If there is in our house

---

[120] Augustine, *Sermones*, 46.5; PL 38:272.

or fellowship someone who is sick, I do not forbid religious men or women to send that person what they think it proper to send," [121] and I do not forbid them to accept it. After all, even the Lord, to whom angels ministered, had a purse, [122] and he accepted things offered by the faithful, and he distributed to his disciples and to other people in need what they required.

Despite what has just been said, solitaries ought to work unceasingly with their own hands, even if they can obtain their livelihood from elsewhere. That is what Paul, the first and the most virtuous of the hermits, did. "When he was in the expanse of the wilderness, he had a reliable supply of food, because he ate only the fruits of palm trees and the berries of plants. Nonetheless, he collected palm leaves and constantly forced himself to complete a daily quota, as though he had to support himself on it. When his cave had become filled with the work of a whole year, he used to take what he had worked at so carefully each year and set it on fire." As has been said, he was not laboring for the food he needed. Rather he acted that way in order to chastise his body, to cleanse his heart, to steady his thoughts, and to persevere in his cell. He used to say that, "without manual work, a solitary cannot continue staying in one place or ever reach the peak of perfection." [123]

Just the opposite was another

brother who came to Abba Silvanus on Mount Sinai. When he saw the brothers working, he said to them: "Do not work for the food that perishes but for the food that endures unto eternal life" [John 6:27]. "Mary has chosen the best part" [Luke 10:42]. So the elder said to his disciple: Go and call that brother, and put him in a cell with nothing in it. When the ninth hour arrived, that brother hurried to the door to see whether the others would send and call him to eat. And when

---

[121] Ibid., 356.13; PL 39:1580.

[122] *loculos.* In John 12:6 we read that Judas kept the common purse, *loculos habens.*

[123] John Cassian, *De institutis coenobiorum*, 10.24; PL 49:394–96. Where Cassian has *monachum*, Grimlaicus has substituted *solitarium*. This same story is also told in *Vitae patrum*, 4.40; PL 73:839, in somewhat shortened form. Grimlaicus' text is closer to Cassian's.

no one spoke to him, he got up and came to the elder and
said to him: Abba, have the brothers eaten today? And the elder
said to him: Yes, they have already eaten. So he said: And why
didn't you call me? The elder responded: You are a spiritual
person, and you don't need this sort of food. We on the other
hand are carnal and want to eat. That is why we work with
our hands. But you, you have chosen the good part; all day
long you read and do not want to eat carnal food. When the
brother had heard this, he prostrated himself on the ground
and humbly did penance and said: Forgive me, abba. And the
elder said to him: I think that Mary certainly needed Martha.
It is through Martha that Mary is praised.[124]

So we see that solitaries need to labor with their hands and to work
for what they eat, because people who enjoy leisurely quiet, unless
they alternate it with manual work and unless they live spiritually,
are living the lives of cattle.

Now if any of the things made by solitaries are to be sold, the
people through whose hands they are to pass must make sure that
they not dare to practice any fraud. Let them always remember
Ananias and Sapphira, lest they suffer in their soul the death that
those two incurred in their bodies [see Acts 5:1ff.]. With regard to
prices, the evil of avarice must not creep in. Rather, items should
always be offered somewhat more cheaply than other people who
are seculars can offer them, "so that in everything God may be
glorified" [1 Pet 4:11].[125]

Chapter 40: At Certain Hours Solitaries Should Be Occupied in Manual Labor[126]

Therefore solitaries should be occupied at certain set times in
prayer and reading and at certain other times in manual labor. This
is the way we propose to order both of these times: The whole

---

[124] *Vitae patrum*, 5.10.69; PL 73:924.
[125] This last paragraph repeats with some changes RB 57.4-9.
[126] Much of this chapter depends on RB 48.7-25.

time from dawn until almost the third hour [127] they should devote to prayer and reading. From the third hour until about the ninth hour they should do whatever work is necessary, unless, during the summer, they want to rest for a little while on their beds, and they should always be combining prayer with their work. From the ninth hour until evening they should again devote themselves to prayer and reading. If the circumstances of the locale or poverty demands it, they should spend more time in manual labor. But everything should be done with moderation, on account of the fainthearted.

On Sundays and feast days, they are to devote themselves only to prayer and reading. Likewise, at night they are to perform the sacred vigils and most pure prayers with the greatest devotion.

Solitaries who are weak[128] should do work that will keep them from being idle but that will not burden them with strenuous exertion. But those who are so sick or who are so weighed down by old age that they can neither read nor work should apply themselves with the greatest devotion, insofar as their strength permits, to prayer alone. Above all, we urge that if someone is not satisfied with this arrangement, that person should draw up a plan that seems more satisfactory.[129]

We will say in what follows, through God's mercy, at what hours they should take their meals.

---

[127] The day was divided into twelve equal parts, beginning at sunrise and ending at sundown. The Latin phrases *ad tertiam, ad sextam, ad nonam, ad vesperam* refer in the first place to the third, sixth, ninth, and evening hours. In monastic terminology, they also stand for the hours of the Divine Office that are celebrated at those times: Terce, Sext, None, and Vespers.

[128] *infirmi*. It is hard to say who exactly the *infirmi* are since in RB the word refers to those who are weak, both in their constitution and because of disease or injury. At times, *infirmi* refers to those who are suffering from sickness, but often, notably in 64:19, the word clearly refers to those who are lacking in strength: "so that the strong [*fortes*] may have something to strive for and the weak [*infirmi*] nothing to run away from." In the next sentence, "those who are sick" are *infirmati*. See Grimlaicus' chapter 47, where *infirmitas* clearly means "weakness" rather than "sickness," and chapter 48, where the context demands that *infirmi* be rendered "sick, infirm."

[129] See RB 18.22, where Benedict says the same about the psalm distribution for Divine Office.

Chapter 41: Solitaries Should Have Nothing of Their Own and Should Accept the Offerings of the Faithful

Hence solitaries should have nothing of their own, except utensils and the poorest furniture without which they could not live at all. They should get a reasonable amount of food and simple clothing either from their own labor or from the offering of the faithful. Whatever is over and above these things, they should give to the poor. As is indicated in the preceding chapter, they are allowed to accept things that people offer them in order to alleviate their own need and that of the poor. That is why we read in the book of Prosper:

> God wants those who worship him to renounce everything that the world offers, so that, once the craving for worldly things has been eliminated, divine charity may grow in them and reach perfection. Tenth parts and first-fruits, first-born and sacrifices for sin, and votive offerings, things that the Lord commanded to be offered to him, he determined should be distributed among the priests and ministers. Since their necessities of life were to be taken care of by very devoted people, they might minister with free minds to the Creator and Shepherd himself and might make progress in his worship and not be hindered by any bodily anxiety. If they were involved in earthly affairs, they would not be able to keep unremitting guard over their office.[130]

In this same work we also read that Saint Paulinus and blessed Hilary either left everything they had to their families or sold it and disbursed the proceeds to the poor. Yet later, when they had been made bishops, they did not despise the church's resources but dispensed them very faithfully.

> These men who were so holy, these prelates who were so perfect, cry out by their manifest deeds that we can and should do what they did. These people were without doubt very

---

[130] Julianus Pomerius, *De Vita Contemplativa*, 2.16.3; PL 59:461.

learned in both secular and divine letters. If they, who had left
all their own possessions, had thought that the church's possessions should be despised, they would never have kept them.
Therefore we are given to understand that so many great
people, who desired to become disciples of Christ, renounced
everything they had in order to possess the church's resources,
not as owners but as administrators. Hence they knew that the
church's property was nothing other than the votive offerings
of the faithful, the price paid by sinners, and the patrimony
of the poor. They did not lay claim to church property for
their own use, as though it belonged to them. They regarded
it as entrusted to them, and they divided it up among the
poor.[131]

It also says, "when a priest accepts from the people whatever
is to be distributed, he is not only without covetousness but also
earns praise for his piety. He is trustworthy in dispensing what he
has received, because he has either left all his own possessions or
has combined them with what the church owns. In his love of
poverty, he counts himself in the number of the poor, and, like a
poor man, he voluntarily lives from the resources with which he
assists the poor."[132]

About this same matter, we read in the Rule for Canons:
"Monks and solitaries, who have followed the gospel precept by
renouncing and parting from everything, have surrendered their
patrimony to Christ. Therefore it is right that they receive temporal
support from the resources of the church. Because they long for
heavenly things with the whole desire of their mind, they should
be supported in this pilgrimage at the Lord's expense, so that their
need for some necessity may in no way compel them to turn back
to what they have rejected."[133] It also says there: "Clerics living in
community, who are poor either voluntarily or by birth, are to
receive the necessities of life, because it was not a craving to possess

---

[131] Ibid., 2.9.1-2; PL 59:453–54.

[132] Ibid., 2.11; PL 59:455.

[133] Amalarius of Metz, *Regula Canonicorum*, 1.115; PL 105:914.

that led them to accept such things. Rather they were forced to do so in order to live."[134]

Further, if there be some who do not want to have either their own or the church's possessions, then prelates ought to exercise providential oversight and supply what they need out of the church's resources. The prelates should note what Prosper says: "What the church has, let it have in common with all who have nothing."[135] They should exercise no less care for those who are burdened by sickness and old age.

After having treated these matters, we must keep in mind what we read in the Acts of the Apostles: "They brought the price of their estates and placed them at the feet of the apostles. These were distributed to each individually, according as each one had need" [Acts 4:34-35]. And: "There was no one among them who was in need" [Acts 4:34]. And also: "No one called anything his or her own, but they held everything in common" [Acts 4:32]. Therefore solitaries should not call anything their own but should be trustworthy distributors. The things that they ought to give to the poor they should by no means turn to their own use. If they do, then—may it never happen—with Judas, who stole from the Lord's purse, they will incur the sentence of damnation. Rather, they should deserve to receive a reward beyond description for their faithful administration from the One whose ministers they are known to be.

Chapter 42: The Hours at Which Solitaries Ought to Take Their Meals

I believe it should be established at what hours solitaries should take their meals. Otherwise some might follow their own will and live in more lax a manner than need be. Consequently, I judge that both mealtimes may be arranged as follows. From the octave of Easter to Pentecost, they should eat twice a day. During these days, therefore, let them fast on Wednesdays and Fridays until mid-afternoon, because, just as reins are put in the mouths of horses, so

---

[134] Ibid., 1.118; PL 105:897.
[135] Julianus Pomerius, *De Vita Contemplativa*, 2.9.2; PL 59:454.

our bodies should be reined in by fasts. From Pentecost to the first of September, they should fast on Wednesdays, Fridays, and Saturdays until mid-afternoon. On the remaining days, let them take their meal at noon and take supper toward evening. From the first of September until the beginning of Lent, they should always take their meal in mid-afternoon, unless perhaps someone wants to prolong the fast until evening. During Lent until Easter, they should take their meal toward evening. Vespers, however, should be so arranged that they do not need lamplight while they eat but may finish everything while it is still daylight. During every season, the hour of the main meal or of supper should be so adjusted that everything may be done by daylight.[136] Furthermore, those who may want to fast during every season, except on Sundays and other feast days, should not be forbidden to do so, since that is what our holy fathers Antony and Benedict did, and also Macarius and others.

In every season, the life of solitaries ought to keep a Lenten observance. But since this sort of virtue is found in few people, we therefore urge that during the days of Lent they guard their life in all purity and wash away during these holy days all the negligences of the other seasons. The right way to do this is to abstain from all evil habits and to devote ourselves to prayer with tears, to reading, to compunction of heart, and to the work of abstinence. Therefore, during these days, let us increase somewhat the usual measure of our service: private prayers and abstinence from food and drink. In this way let each of us offer to God something above and beyond the amount assigned us and do so of our own free will and in the joy of the Holy Spirit; that is to say, let us deprive our body of food and drink, of sleep and rest, of talking and joking, and with the joy of spiritual desire let us look forward to holy Easter.[137]

Finally, in every season, as soon as they get up from the meal, whether it be the noonday meal or supper, let them sit, if there are two of them together, and let one of them read the conferences or lives of the fathers or something else that will edify them. When

---

[136] Much of the foregoing depends on RB 41.
[137] This paragraph follows, almost word for word, RB 49.1-8.

four or five pages have been read, or however much time permits, if it is midday, they may either rest a little on their beds or do some form of manual labor. During the season of the fast, however, when the reading has been finished, if Vespers has already taken place, as soon as they get up from the reading, let them go to celebrate Compline. As they are leaving Compline, let them say nothing further at all, unless, due to some necessity, the superior or one of the brothers wants to tell someone something. But this must be done with the utmost seriousness and appropriate restraint. If, however, a solitary is alone, he should do the same. Indeed, at all times solitaries should be very conscious of keeping silence, especially during the night hours.[138] If one of them wants to pray privately during the night or to do something else, let him do it so as not to disturb the other.[139]

Chapter 43: The Table of Solitaries

Whenever solitaries have enough to eat and drink, either from their own labor or from what the faithful have offered, they should always invite to their table the poor and pilgrims, and they should know that Christ is a guest along with them. If there are no poor, then it is up to them whichever of the brothers it seems good to them in charity to invite. Let them, in all charity, set before those they have invited whatever God may have given them. For their part, solitaries should guard themselves not only against eating choice foods but also against eating too much. When they do not have guests, let them live by weighing and measuring what they eat. But when there are others together with them, they should avoid vainglory and show that they observe normal customs in matters of food and drink. Yet they should not go beyond what is set down in the rule.

---

[138] The foregoing treatment regarding silence depends, with several additions, omissions, and inversions, on RB 42.

[139] This stipulation is an adaptation to the night hours of a regulation in RB 48.5 for the siesta after the midday meal.

We believe that two cooked dishes are sufficient for the daily meal, to allow for the weaknesses of different people, so that those who cannot eat one kind of food may make their meal from the other. And if there is fruit or fresh vegetables, then a third dish may be added. This is what their food should be like: sometimes greens and vegetables, sometimes cheese and eggs, and occasionally, as a great delicacy, they may have small fish. Jerome says: "What you don't taste after swallowing is the same as bread and vegetables to you."[140]

Let a full pound of bread be enough for a day, whether there is one meal or whether there is both a midday meal and supper. Some people need more, and some less, since different bodies are endowed with differing strength. It is not easy for us to debate the quality and amount of food, since all people cannot hold to one uniform rule. Nonetheless, they must make every effort not always to finish eating because they are full but because they want to. Overeating should not stuff the stomach; rather, undereating should shrink it. This is what the Apostle is referring to: "Do not take care of the flesh in its desires" [Rom 13:14]. He did not prohibit every and all care of the flesh; he only forbade us to cater to its desires.

They are to abstain entirely from the meat both of four-footed animals and of fowl. But those in the grip of a severe illness are allowed to eat meat only to help them recuperate. Once they have become stronger, they are to abstain from meat as usual.[141]

Chapter 44: Avoiding Overindulgence

Insofar as they are able, therefore, solitaries should flee from delicacies and from an overabundance of food. They should keep themselves, not only from wanting expensive food, but also from eating too much common food. Above all, overindulgence is to be avoided, lest indigestion overtake them, since nothing is so unbecoming any Christian as overindulgence. Hence the Lord says:

---

[140] Jerome, Ep 58.6; PL 22:583.
[141] The second, third, and fourth paragraphs of this chapter reflect the arrangements of RB 39.

"Watch out that your hearts be not weighed down by overindulgence and drunkenness" [Luke 21:34].[142] Nothing so inflames and
excites the genital members as does digested food and the convul-
sion of belching. Many foods weaken not only our hearts but also
our bodies and souls. Often, through our eagerness to eat, the
stomach's natural strength is ruined, and because of the overabundance of food, we suffer an excess of blood, jaundice, and many
diseases. Consequently we should each allow ourselves as much
food as the body requires for its sustenance, not as much as the
desire of the flesh demands. It is fitting, therefore, that our flesh be
subject to our soul, just as a handmaid is subservient to her lady.
When our stomach is loaded with food, we cannot keep vigil
properly, but sleep lies heavy on us. We lose the fruit of the vigils
and inflict the greatest harm on our soul. Just as a soldier is weighed
down by too heavy a load and is impeded from fighting, so solitaries
are impeded from vigils when they are hot and flushed from having
eaten too much.

The devil is overjoyed when he sees God's servants stuffed with
too much food, as we read concerning a certain venerable man,
Saint Philibert. When he was in a certain monastery and had taken
upon himself Christ's sweet yoke and light burden, he made such
progress in religious observance that he became an example even
to the men who were the most perfect in abstinence and in the
other virtues. Now since his ancient enemy begrudged him this
abstinence, on a certain day he assaulted Philibert's resolve[143] so
that he ate more than enough food. Afterward, that very night,
while he was surfeited with food, it pleased God to disclose the
enemy and show him to Saint Philibert in a dream. The devil began
to pat the saint's belly gleefully and say, "Everything's fine here,
everything's fine here." Then the Lord's soldier recognized the
missiles of the enemy. He fortified himself with the rampart of the
cross and devoted himself to trebling the rigor of his abstinence.[144]
This incident shows the kind and extent of the traps the enemy

---

[142] See RB 39.8-9.
[143] *animus*
[144] The source of this story about Philibert could not be located.

uses to try to trip up God's servants and how glad he is made by overeating.

Therefore let us so strive to restrain our eating that, even if the enemy should at some time have had reason to rejoice at our overeating, he may be turned back in confusion because of our abstinence. Everything should be done in due measure and with discretion, because too much abstinence from foods not only breaks the powers of the body but also diminishes the attention of the soul. It enfeebles the mind's ability to think and saps the vitality of prayer. Consequently whatever is done in due proportion is salutary; what is done in excess and beyond due measure is harmful and turns enthusiasm for something into its opposite. That is why Saint Anthony said: "There are those who beat their body down through abstinence, but since they do not have discretion, they move far away from God." [145] On this same topic, blessed Gregory says: It often happens that, "when someone wears down the flesh through abstinence more than is necessary, that person appears outwardly humble, but that very humility leads the person to be inwardly extremely proud. Hence those who are abstaining must be warned to pay close attention to themselves and make sure that, while they are fleeing from the vice of gluttony, they do not fall into pride or vainglory." [146] Conversely, they must be warned always to guard their abstinence without changing it and never to believe that their abstinence is a matter of extreme virtue before the secret Judge. If they do, then they might think they deserve a great reward, and their hearts might get carried away with self-exaltation. Let us, then, chastise our bodies and also the promptings of our bodies with the rigor of very strict abstinence in such a way that we may be cleansed from carnal desires and may flower with holy virtues.

---

[145] *Vitae patrum*, 5.10.1; PL 73:912.
[146] Gregory the Great, *Regula pastoralis*, 3.19; PL 77:82.

Chapter 45: The Amount of Drink of Solitaries[147]

The amount of drink that Saint Benedict established for monks,
that same amount do we, while conscious of the feebleness of the
weak,[148] establish for solitaries, that is, a hemina of wine per day for
each.[149] But those to whom God grants the endurance to abstain
should know that they will have their own reward, as the Apostle
says: "Each person has a special gift from God, one this and another
that" [1 Cor 7:7].

If the poverty of the place or work or weakness demands that
they drink more, they may choose to do so, but in every case they
must take care that excess or drunkenness not creep in. In fact, we
read that wine is not for monks or solitaries, but because in our
days monks and solitaries cannot be convinced of this, let us at least
agree that they not drink to excess but sparingly, because wine
makes apostates even of the wise [see Sir 19:2]. But when the
poverty of the place dictates that not even the abovementioned
measure can be found, but much less, or even none at all, let those
who live there bless God and not be sad; rather, they should rejoice
at being free of such a plague. Above all, we admonish them to
keep from grumbling.

Concerning abstinence from wine, the Apostle set down this
fixed rule: "Do not get drunk on wine, in which is debauchery"
[Eph 5:18]. It is as though he said, it is not nature but drinking too
much wine that begets and feeds debauchery. Hence, I do not
forbid solitaries to use wine, but I do forbid them to get drunk.
Granted that a moderate use of wine makes a weak stomach stronger, nonetheless drunkenness weakens both spirit[150] and body.
Finally, the Apostle commands his disciple Timothy: "Do not drink
just water, but use a little wine, on account of your stomach pain
and on account of your frequent illnesses" [1 Tim 5:23]. This shows
that those who take wine, not to get drunk but only for the sake

---

[147] The first two paragraphs of this chapter follow RB 40 closely.

[148] See note 128 above.

[149] *RB 1980* translates the Latin *hemina* as "a half bottle" (note 40.3 on p. 238).
Estimates vary. Kardong (p. 329) opts for the *hemina* being about a half quart.

[150] *animus*

of the body's health, are not acting against abstinence. This is not offered to them by their will but permitted to them by their weakness. But if they are not weak, they should abstain from wine, so that the drinking of wine, which sustains a weak body, does not set a healthy one on fire.[151]

Surely no one has said that it is a sin to use wine and to make use of oil, but in those regions where there is no oil, fat may sometimes be used, if necessary.

Chapter 46: Avoiding Drunkenness, and the Praise of Sobriety

Above all, solitaries are to avoid the vice of drunkenness, since it is written: A drunkard is the slave of every vice.[152] The person who is held captive by much wine does not have the strength to overcome a single sin. That is why Solomon said: "A wanton thing is wine, and drunkenness brings uproar. Whoever delights in them will not be wise" [Prov 20:1], and also: "Do not gaze at wine when its golden color shines in the glass. It goes down smoothly, but it ends up biting like a snake, and like a serpent it pours out its venom" [Prov 23:31-32]. "Where drunkenness reigns, there is no secret" [Prov 31:4]. On this subject blessed Jerome says: "Drunkenness is always the mother of disgraceful actions, the root of crimes, the occasion of faults, and the origin of all vices."[153] "A stomach burning with wine quickly foams over in lustful desires."[154] Therefore let us flee from drunkenness, lest we fall into the sin of debauchery.

---

[151] In 1 Tim 5:23, *infirmitates* probably means "illnesses," yet the tenor of this chapter seems to warrant that, in these final lines too, *infirmitas* be rendered "weakness."

[152] Source not located.

[153] Sedulius Scotus, *Collectaneum miscellaneum*, 8.5.3; CCCM 67:59–60. Sedulius gives this saying under Jerome's name, but the source could not be located.

[154] Jerome, Ep 69.9; PL 22:663. This saying is also found in Sedulius Scotus, *Collectaneum miscellaneum*, 13.5.4; CCCM 67:60.

By drinking wine, many people have brought on themselves great bodily infirmity and could not regain their former health, because they did not restrain the ardor of their appetite. By over-indulging in wine, the mouth is armed to pronounce curses and to wrangle with one's neighbors; the mind gets befuddled, and the tongue babbles. When this kind of man thinks he is drinking, he is actually getting drunk. Just as a fish that hastens with greedy jaws to swallow the bait suddenly finds the hook in its mouth, so does the drunkard take his enemy, wine, into himself, and, alas! a rational human being is caught like an irrational animal. Nothing is more obviously a demon than drunkenness. Therefore let us drink, not as much as appetite demands, but as much as the frailty of our nature requires. The Lord created wine for us, not to get drunk on but to gladden our hearts [see Ps 103:15]. For just as drunkenness is the mother of every vice, so sobriety is the mother of every virtue. Indeed sobriety is medicine that is beneficial to both body and soul. It preserves memory, renders the senses more acute, cleanses the mind, tames vices, shatters lust, extends old age, reveals the secrets of the divine Sacrament, and makes a person chaste and steadfast in everything. And so, in everything let us show that we are sober, so that through everything sobriety may show that we are healthy and chaste.

Chapter 47: Whether Everyone Should Receive in Equal Measure the Necessities of Life

Blessed Augustine, a man discreet in every matter, says: "Food and clothing should not be given to everyone in equal measure, but rather as each one has need. Likewise we read in the Acts of the Apostles: 'These were distributed, according as each one had need,'"[155] "and among them no one was needy" [Acts 4:34-35]. By this we are not saying that with God there is regard for persons but rather consideration for weaknesses. Thus those who need less should thank God, whereas those who need more should be hum-bled by their weakness and not become haughty because of the

---

[155] Augustine, Ep 211.5; PL 33:960.

mercy they have received. They too should thank God, since God is to be blessed in everything.[156]

On this subject, there is an example in the conferences of the fathers. Even though it is lengthy, still I think it is beneficial in this connection.

> Once there came a monk from the city of Rome, who had a high position in the palace, and he used to dwell in Scete near the church. Now he had with him one of his servants, who took care of his needs. The priest of the church, seeing the man's weakness and realizing that he was used to fine things, used to send him part of what God granted him. When he had lived this way in Scete for twenty-five years, he became a most renowned contemplative, that is, one who had spiritual sight. One of the great monks of Egypt heard of his reputation and came to see him in the hope of finding an even sterner bodily observance.[157] When this monk entered, the other greeted him, and they prayed together and sat down. When the Egyptian saw that he was clothed in soft garments and had a fleece laid out under him and a little pillow under his head, and that he had clean feet with little shoes, he was scandalized at him within himself, because in that place it was not the custom to follow that sort of observance but on the contrary to observe rigorous abstinence. Now the Roman elder had contemplation, that is, the grace of spiritual sight, and he understood that the Egyptian monk had become scandalized at him, so he said to his servant: Make today a special day because of the abba who has come. He cooked the few vegetables that he had, and they arose at a suitable hour and ate. The elder also had a little wine on account of his weakness, and they drank it. And when evening came on, they said twelve psalms and went to sleep. They did the same at night. When they got up in the morning, the Egyptian said to him: Pray for me, and he left, not edified at him. When he had gone off

---

[156] The first paragraph of this chapter, apart from the quotation from Saint Augustine, depends on RB 34.

[157] *corporalem conversationem.* Here and in the second sentence below, *conversatio* seems to have a meaning narrower than simply "way of life."

a little way, the Roman elder, wishing to cure him, sent after him and called him back. When he had come, he once again received him joyfully.

He asked him: What province do you come from? He answered: I am Egyptian.

And he said: From what city? But he responded: I am not from a city at all, and I haven't ever lived in one.

The elder said to him: Before you became a monk, what sort of work did you do on the estate where you lived? He responded: I used to tend the fields.

He said to him: Where did you sleep? The Egyptian responded: In the field.

The Roman asked: Did you have any sort of bed? He said: How could I have had bedding in the field?

The elder asked: How did you sleep? The Egyptian responded: On the bare ground.

The Roman said: What did you used to eat in the field or what kind of wine did you drink? He said: I used to eat dry bread and any salted food that I found, and I used to drink water.

To these answers the Roman elder said: That cost you a great deal of labor. And he added: Was there on the estate a bath where you might wash? The Egyptian said: No, but when I wanted to, I used to wash in the river.

When therefore the elder had asked him all these things and had found out how he used to live and work, he wanted to gain him some benefit, and so he told him about his past life and how he lived while he was a secular. He said: My miserable self, whom you see, am from the great city of Rome. In the palace I had an important position with the emperor. When the Egyptian had heard the first of his words, he was at once seized with compunction and listened very attentively to what the other was saying.

The elder went on: And so I left Rome and came into this solitude. He continued: This person whom you see had spacious, large houses and a great deal of money, but I despised them and came to stay in this little lopsided cell. Now keep listening: in addition I had beds covered with gold and very expensive bedclothes, and in place of these God has given me this mat of papyrus and this fleece. My garments were beyond price, and in place of them I use these poor little things. Plenty of gold was expended to buy my food, and in place of that God has given me these few vegetables and this little cup of wine. Numerous servants used to be at my service, and in place of them all God has made this one feel so sorry for me that he takes care of my needs. In place of a deep bath, I use a little water for my feet and little shoes, on account of my weakness. Furthermore, in place of reed pipes and cithara and other instruments that I used to enjoy at my banquets I chant twelve psalms a day, and I do the same at night. For the sins that I committed before, I offer to God my small service. And so I ask you, abba, not to be scandalized at my weakness.

When the Egyptian had heard these things and had come to his senses, he said: Woe is me, because from great hardship and labor in the world I have come to a monk's way of life[158] and enjoy rest, and the things that I didn't have before I now have. You, on the other hand, have left many delights in the world and, by your own free will, have come into this hardship. You have left much glory and abundant wealth and have laid hold of this humility and poverty.

The Egyptian derived great profit from the experience, said good-bye and departed. From then on, he became his friend and used to come to him to benefit from him. That Roman was discerning about what is good, and he was filled with the best aroma of the Holy Spirit.[159]

Thus we see that great discretion is needed between nobles and non-nobles, between robust and weak,[160] between old and young. Those who come from the world's pleasures and those who have never experienced them cannot keep to the same strictness of abstinence. The robust and the weak cannot abstain to the same extent. Consequently we must follow the Apostle's advice: "The one who does not eat is not to scorn the one who does eat, and the one who eats is not to judge the one who does not eat" [Rom 14:3]. Rather, they should lovingly support one another and take one another's weaknesses into account.

---

[158] *in conversationem monachi*
[159] *Vitae patrum*, 5.10.76; PL 73:925.
[160] *infirmus*. See note 128.

Chapter 48: Solitaries Who Are Sick and Old[161]

Above and before anything else, care is to be taken of the sick and the old, so that they are served just as Christ would be. At the judgment, he himself will say to the just: "I was sick and you visited me," and: "What you did to one of my least, you did to me" [Matt 25:36, 40]. But those who are frail and sick should realize that they are being served for the honor of God and not distress the brothers who are serving them by their excessive demands or frivolous words. But even if they are very demanding, still they must be patiently borne with, because it is from such as these that a more ample reward is gained in the kingdom of God. Therefore the superiors and the other brothers are to be extremely careful that the sick suffer no neglect. They should support them by their compassion, by constant visits, by the consolations of the Holy Scriptures, and they should provide them out of their own resources with the support they need.

Let a brother be designated, one who is God-fearing, attentive, and responsible. He is to be compassionate in dispensing to them what they need and offer them the use of baths as often as is appropriate. If they wish, they may eat meat to restore their health, but only until they are better.

The cells of the sick, during the time of their infirmity, are not to be kept under seal, so that they can be visited by the brothers. Nevertheless they must take care not to go out past the established limit, if they were enclosed and sealed by the bishop, for it is not a seal of wax or lead that holds them, but the seal of Christ. In the Book of Dialogues we read what a certain venerable man, named Martin, did.

> When he was dwelling on a certain mountain in a cave that had not been sealed, he fastened his foot with an iron chain and attached the other end of it to a rock. That way he could go no further than the length of the chain. When Benedict, the man of venerable life, heard this, he made it his business

---

[161] Much of the matter of this chapter, apart from the story of Martin, is drawn from RB 36 and 37.

to send his disciple to him with this command: If you are a servant of Christ, do not hold yourself with a chain of iron but with the chain of Christ. When he heard this message, Martin at once undid that fetter, but ever afterwards he never set foot beyond the place where he used to reach when his foot was shackled. He continued to keep himself confined in the same space in which before he stayed when he was tied.[162]

That is how recluses should act. However, as soon as they begin to recover from their illness, the door of the cell should be sealed in the customary manner, and they should dwell alone once more.

As we have said, the superior must take great care that the old and the sick are not neglected by the cellarer, since masters are responsible for whatever their disciples fail to do. Their frailty must always be taken into account, and the strictness of the rule is certainly not to be applied to them with regard to foods or other necessities. Rather, loving consideration must be shown them, and they should, if necessary, anticipate the canonical hours.

Chapter 49: The Clothing and Footwear of Solitaries

It is incumbent upon solitaries to obey the authority of the Holy Scriptures and to be vigilant in reflecting upon the examples of the holy fathers, so that the humility they carry in their heart they may most devoutly show forth in deed, in clothing, even in their way of walking. They should want to shine more by their holy way of life and exceptional conduct than by the embellishment of their clothes. How much they ought to restrain themselves from superfluous and excessive attention to clothing may be learned from many examples of the holy fathers.

Blessed Gregory says: "Do not think that you can be without sin in lusting and craving for expensive clothes, because, if this were not a sin, then the Lord would not have praised John for the austerity of his clothing" [see Matt 11:8].[163] And he also says: "No

---

[162] Gregory the Great, *Dialogorum libri*, 3.16; PL 77:261.
[163] Gregory the Great, *XL Homiliae in Evangelia*, 1.6.3; PL 76:1097.

one desires to wear special clothing except to win empty glory,
that is, to seem to be more honorable than others. People do not
want to put on expensive clothes in a place where they cannot be
seen by others. We desire to wear expensive garments only to gain
empty glory." [164]

On this same topic Basil said: "If we are really striving to be
the least of all and the last of all, we should certainly think that we
are last of all in clothing too." [165] And Cassian says: The clothing of
a solitary should be of such a kind "that it clothes the body and
simply covers the shame of nudity and keeps off injurious cold but
does not feed any occasion of vanity. It should be so ordinary that
no novelty of color or style makes it stand out among the other
spiritual brothers." [166] And Isidore says: The garments of solitaries
are neither very poor nor very expensive, since a very "expensive
garment draws a person[167] toward lewdness, while one that is too
poor either engenders sorrow of heart or gives rise to the malady
of vainglory." [168]

Thus far we have been speaking about the quality of clothing.
Now, however, let us say something about its quantity. Solitaries
should not have many or superfluous garments. They should
imitate the saying of our God to his disciples: "You are not to have
two tunics" [Luke 9:3]. We should not take these "two tunics" as
referring to the number two. What it means is that if we are wearing some things and are keeping other things because of avarice,
then these latter are superfluous, and we are commanded to give
them to the poor. That is why Saint Jerome says: "Whatever can
protect our bodies and assist our human frailty, that may be called
one tunic, and whatever we require by way of immediate nourish-
ment, that is called food for one day. That is what the precept from

---

[164] Ibid., 2.40.3; PL 76:1305. Grimlaicus' phrasing is closer to the version of
Gregory's words cited in Defensor, 42.9.

[165] Basil, *Regula*, 11, as found in the *Codex regularum* (PL 103:502–3). This
passage is also found in Benedict of Aniane's *Concordia regularum*, 62.4; PL 103:1239.

[166] John Cassian, *De institutis coenobiorum*, 1.3; PL 49:64–65.

[167] *animus*. The text of Isidore's rule as it appears in PL 103 has *anima*, but in
PL 83 *animus*.

[168] Isidore of Seville, *Regula monachorum*, 13; PL 103:566, and also PL 83:881,
where it is 12.

the Lord means, that we not think about tomorrow, that is, about the future [see Matt 6:34]. And the Apostle says: 'If we have food and clothing, let us be content with these.' "[169] "For those who want to become rich are falling into temptation and into the devil's snare and into many useless and harmful desires that plunge a person down to ruin and destruction" [1 Tim 6:8-9].

For this reason, we have recourse to the rule of blessed Benedict,[170] and we allow solitaries to have as much clothing as he allows monks to have. That is to say, to allow for night wear and for washing the clothes, if they are monks, they should have two tunics and two cowls. If however they have not yet taken on the monastic manner of life, they should not wear cowls but capes, thin in summer, wooly in winter. They should have one fur-lined cloak, two woven undergarments, and two pair of leggings. Anyone is to be allowed to use leggings, especially those who are involved with the ministry of the altar. However, the other grades of clergy may determine for themselves whether or not they want to wear them. They are also to have footwear: boots, shoes, and sandals. They should rely on their own judgment to see to it that they have garments that suit the nature of the locality and the climate, because in cold regions more is needed than in warm regions. Furthermore, priests are to take special care to keep the priestly vestments and altar linens clean, that is to say, each one is to have one chasuble, two albs, two amices, two stoles with maniples, and also two corporals and two linen cloths. They are to keep these items clean, as befits such a ministry.

Chapter 50: The Bedding of Solitaries

As in other matters, so too with regard to their bedding, solitaries should keep to the norm of discretion, namely, they should not want to have expensive bedding but cheap. Their clothing and footwear and their bedding should be neither excessively tidy nor overly shabby. As we have said, they should keep to the virtue of

---

[169] Jerome, Ep 120; PL 22:985. Jerome's citation of 1 Tim ends after this first sentence. The first part of this citation of Jerome is also found in Defensor, 42.8.
[170] See RB 55.

discretion and steer between the two extremes. Let these things suffice for their bedding: a mat and goat-hair covering, a woolen blanket or thick coverlet, and a pillow. They are to sleep clothed and with their belts on, so that they may always be ready.[171] As they rest on their beds, they are to repeat frequently with the prophet: "Every night I will wash my bed, I will water my couch with my tears" [Ps 6:7]. And also: "At night I remembered your name, O Lord, and I kept your law" [Ps 118:55].

If they have not already arisen, they should arise without delay when the signal is given and hasten to the work of God, yet with all gravity and decorum. When they have arisen, they should first make the sign of the cross on their foreheads and say silently: "O God, come to my assistance; O Lord, make haste to help me" [Ps 69:1]. As they chant this verse, let them proceed at once to the oratory. As they lie prostrate on the ground, let them humbly pray with tears and sighs. When they have finished praying,[172] they should take care of the needs of nature. When they have returned to the oratory, they are to begin the night office solemnly and reverently. When they are leaving to go somewhere else or when they are returning, they should always be chanting some part of the Psalter with mouth and heart, so that they may be able confidently to say with the prophet: "I will bless the Lord at every time, his praise always in my mouth" [Ps 33:1].

Chapter 51: They Should Shave at Certain Times, so as Not to Be Hairy.

In shaving their beards and trimming their hair, solitaries should keep to the norm of discretion. We read in the lives of the fathers that there was a certain holy man named Apollonius,

> who scolded severely those who let their beard and hair grow
> long. He used to say: It is certain that these people are seeking

---

[171] See RB 22.5-6.

[172] The *oratio* or prayer being spoken of at this point is private, silent prayer. See RB 20 and *RB 1980*, 412–13.

praise from human beings, and they are letting their beard and hair grow long in order to show off, even though we are commanded to celebrate even our fasts in private, so that they may be known only to God who sees what is in private and who repays in public. But it seems to me that these people are not content with being repaid by the One who sees in private but want to display themselves to human beings.[173]

Similarly it is said that blessed Gregory spoke this proverb to a certain Roman: "If holiness were in a beard, then no one would be holier than a goat."[174]

Consequently, I regard it as reasonable and fitting that solitaries, and especially those who handle the sacred Mysteries, shave and trim their hair every forty days, as the Apostle says: Let us "scour off the old human being with its deeds and put on the one who is renewed unto knowledge of God" [Col 3:9-10], that is, let us strip off the sins of our flesh like the hairs of our head,[175] and so let us shine with our senses renewed. This renewal ought to take place in our mind, but it ought also to be shown on our head, where the mind is thought to dwell.

Inside the cell of their reclusion they should also have a tub, and as often as appropriate, the priests should make use of baths to cleanse their bodies. But perhaps some people might say: Saint Anthony never took a bath. These people may be answered in a few words: Saint Anthony may never have taken a bath, but neither did he ever sing the Mass. And so the taking of baths is left up to the priests, so that they may be clean and worthy when they celebrate the sacred Mysteries.

---

[173] Rufinus: *Historia Monachorum*, 7, "*de Apollonio;*" PL 21:419

[174] There were Greek and Latin epigrams about goats, beards, and wisdom, but the wisecrack in this wording first surfaces in Eugene of Toledo's *Carmen* 89 (MGH, *Auctores antiquissimi*, 14, 266). See Giles Constable, intro. to *Apologia de barbis* of Burchhardt of Bellevaux, in *Apologiae duae*, ed. R. B. C. Huygens, CCCM, 62.121 (Brepols: Turnhout, 1985), 121.

[175] Grimlaicus here plays with the similar sounds of *criminibus*, "sins," and *crinibus*, "hairs."

Chapter 52: The Disciples of Solitaries and Their Obedience[176]

Disciples of solitaries should often be admonished to live in such a way that they may give others good example and humbly submit to the commands of their masters. Therefore, as soon as something is commanded them by their masters, as though the command came from God, they permit themselves no delay in doing it. But this obedience will be acceptable to God and pleasing to human beings only if what is ordered is carried out neither tardily nor tepidly nor with the response of someone who is unwilling. Indeed obedience that is rendered to superiors is shown to God, for he himself said: "Whoever hears you hears me" [Luke 10:16]. If disciples obey with ill will[177] and grumble, not only with their mouth, but also in their heart, then even though they fulfill the orders of the superior, it will nevertheless not be acceptable to God who observes the heart of the grumbler. For such a deed, they will gain no merit. On the contrary, they will incur the penalty due to grumblers, unless they make satisfaction and improve.

And so such people immediately put aside their own affairs and relinquish their own will, as the Lord declared: "I have come not to do my own will but that of the One who sent me" [John 6:38]. They drop what they have, leave unfinished what they were doing, and, with the lively step of obedience, they follow up with actions the voice of the one who commands them.

An example of this is given in the conferences of the fathers:

> Abba Sylvanus had a disciple by the name of Mark who excelled in obedience. Now this man was a scribe. The elder loved him because he was so obedient. He also had eleven other disciples who were dejected because the elder loved Mark more than he loved them. When the elders in the area heard that he loved him more than his other disciples, they took offense. Now one day they came to him. Abba Sylvanus made them welcome and then went out and began to knock

---

[176] The first two paragraphs of this chapter depend heavily on RB 5.
[177] *malo animo*

on the doors of the cells of each one of his disciples, saying: Brother, come, because I need you. Not one of them followed him immediately. But he came to Mark's cell and said to him: Come, brother, because I need you. Now he was writing and did not finish the letter "O" and came. And the elders said: Truly, abba, the one whom you love, we love, because the Lord loves him too.[178]

I have cited this example here that disciples may learn to carry out obedience without delay.

Disciples should not be proud or tardy or unruly or prone to drinking too much wine or to eating too much.[179] Rather they should live honorably and uprightly and fear God. Those who faithfully administer to their masters the things that God has given in their season and who administer them without making their masters sad are keeping in mind the divine saying: "Whoever scandalizes one of the little ones who believe in me," and so on [Matt 18:6-7]. They should also call to mind what the Apostle says: "Whoever ministers well earns a good standing for himself" [1 Tim 3:13], and also: "God loves a cheerful giver" [2 Cor 9:7]. Someone who does not have any resources that have been donated should offer a good word in reply, as it is written: "A good word is above the best gift" [Sir 18:17].[180]

They are to regard all their vessels and resources as though they were the sacred vessels of the altar. They are not to neglect anything. They must not be eager to amass possessions or be wasteful and squander the resources of others. Rather, they should do everything with moderation and according to the orders of the masters.[181]

Solitaries should not want to have many disciples, because they can never overcome avarice when they are intent on supporting many people. Let each one have one or two disciples, or, at most, three. They should, that is, have few disciples who live with them

---

[178] *Vitae patrum*, 5.14.5; PL 73:948.

[179] See RB 4.35 and 31.1, where similar qualities are stipulated for the monastery cellarer.

[180] Sirach is also cited in RB 31.13.

[181] See RB 31.10-12. Again, this description applies to the monastery cellarer.

but many whom they teach. Nonetheless, we are not saying that they should give instruction to all comers, for even though this is permitted, it is not beneficial. That is why the Apostle says: "All things are permitted me, but not all things are beneficial" [1 Cor 6:12].

Chapter 53: Concerning the Good Zeal That Solitaries Ought to Have Toward Their Disciples[182]

As Saint Benedict says: Just as there is a good zeal that separates a person from vices and leads to God and to eternal life, so too there is a zeal of bitterness that separates from God and leads to hell. Toward their disciples solitaries should exercise this zeal that leads to eternal life with the most fervent love. That is, they should be most patient in bearing with their weaknesses, whether of body or of conduct, and if they happen to do something wrong, they should correct them with all moderation.

When they do correct their disciples, they should act prudently and make it their aim to be loved rather than feared. They should not go to extremes, lest in trying to scrape off the rust, the vessel be broken. They should always distrust their own frailty and remember that the bruised reed should not be broken [see Isa 42:3]. In saying this we do not mean that they should permit vices to be fostered, nor should they pretend not to notice the sins of those who do wrong, but as soon as sins begin to arise, they should, insofar as they can, cut them off at the root. They must always remember that Heli the priest was condemned for the wickedness of his sons [see 1 Sam 2:12ff.]. Consequently, let them hold to the advice of the Apostle, who says: "Use argument, plead, rebuke in all patience and teaching" [2 Tim 4:2], that is, use firm argument with the undisciplined; plead with the obedient and gentle to make greater progress; rebuke the negligent and contemptuous, but do everything with patience. But those who are impudent and stubborn and proud, or who are disobedient, if their age permits, they

---

[182] The first part of this chapter depends on RB 72. The second part is a blending of RB 64.12-22 and RB 2.12-14, 23-29.

should curb by chastising them with beatings and with physical punishments, as it is written: "Strike your son with a rod, and you will save his soul from hell" [Prov 23:14]. Above all, they must make sure to provide healing poultices[183] that are right for the kind of wounds. But they should take care that, while they attend to reforming others by their admonitions, they themselves are found to be reformed from all their vices, lest perhaps they preach to others and themselves—may it never happen—turn out to be degenerate [see 1 Cor 9:27].

Chapter 54: How Solitaries Ought to Fast

We need fasts, just as wounds need medication, provided, however, that they are authenticated by the testimony of two things: by prayer and by almsgiving. Thus blessed Augustine says: "It is good to fast, but it is better to give alms. Almsgiving is good by itself without fasting, but fasting is no good by itself without almsgiving. Fasting without almsgiving is like a lamp without oil. And just as a lamp that is lit without having any oil in it can give off smoke but no light, so fasting without almsgiving torments the flesh but does not light up the soul with the light of charity."[184]

But we must investigate how solitaries can be commanded to give alms, since they have offered up to the Lord in faith not only their goods but their very selves. The response comes not from me but from the Lord through the prophet; he says: "Break your bread for the hungry," and so on [Isa 58:7]. He did not say: "Give all your bread to the hungry," but "Break your bread for the hungry." That is why the Apostle says: "It is not that others should be refreshed while you are distressed, but that, by way of balance, your abundance

---

[183] Grimlaicus' image (*exhibeant fomenta curationum*) echoes that of RB 28.3: "if he has provided poultices" (*si exhibuit fomenta*).

[184] These words, attributed to Augustine, are found in Defensor, 10.13, 14, 16. The first two sentences are from Caesarius of Arles, 199.2. The remainder is from the same sermon, 6 [CC 104:804, 806]. These words are also found in PL 83:1219–20, in appendix 12 to the works of Isidore, *sermo primus*: "*Ad carnes tollendas.*"

should provide for the need of others, so that their abundance can then supply your need" [2 Cor 8:13-14]. And elsewhere it is written: "If you have much, give much, but if you have little, you should still give a little" [Tob 4:8-9]. There are three kinds of almsgiving that we should practice unceasingly. "The first is bodily: to give what we can to the needy. The second is spiritual: to forgive someone who has harmed us."[185] The third is to correct those who are doing wrong and to lead those who are straying back into the way of truth. To these three, however, we should join prayer, and then our fasting will be perfect. Thus it was said: "Prayer with fasting is good" [Tob 12:8]. By means of fasts and prayers, mysteries kept concealed in heaven are revealed and secrets known only to God are laid open.

Indeed, no one can reach perfect virtue before mastering the voracious gut. Fasts should be moderate and not weaken the stomach too much, because a moderate and sensible amount of food is good for body and soul. We must ask whether solitaries should fast for two or three days at a time. Blessed Jerome gives this answer: "A small amount of food and a stomach always hungry is preferable to three-day fasts, and it is much better to eat sparingly every day than on rare occasions to eat until you are full. The best rain is the one that falls softly onto the ground; a sudden deluge turns a cultivated field into a gully."[186]

About this matter, we read in the conferences of the fathers:

> Abba Joseph asked Abba Pastor: How should a person fast? He responded: It is good that a monk or solitary eat every day and reduce the amount of food a little so that he doesn't become full. And Abba Joseph said: But when you were young, didn't you fast for two days at a time? The elder said: Believe me, I did, and even for three days or a whole week. But the great elders tested all these things and discovered that is it good

---

[185] Isidore of Seville, *Sententiarum libri*, 3.60.15; PL 83:734. Also: Defensor, 48.41, to which Grimlaicus' wording corresponds.

[186] Jerome, Ep 54.10; PL 22:555. The first part of this quotation is also found in Defensor, 10.22, 25.

to eat every day, but to eat little, so that a person is hungry every day. They pointed out to us this easy royal road.[187]

For fasts of two or three days exhibit vainglory. Another brother posed this question: "What good are the fasts and vigils that a person performs? The elder said to him: These are the things that serve to humble the soul."[188] That is why David used to say: "In fasting I humbled by soul; my prayer is changed in my breast" [Ps 34:13]. We see that our just people and prophets, when they wanted to obtain something from God, used to afflict themselves with fasting, and in this way they rejoiced to obtain what they were asking for. We too should humble our soul by fasting; then we will obtain from God what we request.

Let us not, then, think that we are better than those who cannot fast to the extent that we do; otherwise they may have a greater portion of humility and the other virtues and rightly be thought better than we who are fasting and abstaining. "Bodily fasting will not make us any more perfect unless it is joined to a fast of the soul. The soul has foods that are harmful to it. If it has been fattened on them, then even without eating too much, it goes tumbling down the precipice of excess."[189] Pride, vainglory, slander, envy, and other similar vices—these are the soul's foods. Hence it does us no good to abstain from carnal food and to stuff our breast with foods like these. Consequently, if we want abstinence and fasting to be of any use to us, we must stay clear of these and all vices and strive to climb, with the aid of God's grace, to the peak of the holy virtues.

Chapter 55: Solitaries Should Break Their Fast for the Sake of Guests

Concerning the reception of brothers who come to visit for some charitable reason, blessed Prosper has this to say:

---

[187] *Vitae patrum*, 5.10.44; PL 73:920.

[188] Ibid., 4; PL 73:1015.

[189] John Cassian, *De institutis coenobiorum* 5.21; PL 49:238. The remainder of this chapter also depends on Cassian.

If, on account of people who arrive, I interrupt the fast and eat a meal, then I am not breaking the fast but fulfilling the duty of charity. Conversely, if, for the sake of my abstinence or fast, I sadden spiritual brothers when I know they would have been glad if I relaxed my fast, then my abstinence must be called vice, not virtue. The reason is this: the very abstinence and continuation of fasting, if not set aside when circumstances demand, will puff me up and sadden my brother, whom charity commands me to serve, and will surely demonstrate that there is in me not a trace of heavenly charity.[190]

Hence Saint Benedict says: All guests that arrive should be received like Christ, because he will say: "I was a stranger[191] and you received me" [Matt 25:35]. And proper honor should be shown to "all, especially to members of the household of faith" [Gal 6:10] and to pilgrims.[192] And a little further along he says: The fast should be broken by a monk or solitary for the sake of a guest, unless it happens to be a special fast day that cannot be violated. However, at other times they should observe the customary fasts. But the greatest care and solicitude is to be shown to the poor and especially pilgrims, because especially in them Christ is received. For awe of the wealthy guarantees them honor.

Concerning this matter, the following example is given in the conferences of the fathers:

> Abba Sylvanus had gone with his disciple Zachary to visit a certain monastery. Before they left, the monks made them eat, for the sake of charity. Now it was a fast day. After they had left, the disciple found some water by the road, and he wanted to drink. Abba Sylvanus looked at him and said: Zachary, don't drink. Don't you know that there is a fast today? But the disciple said: But father, didn't we take food today at the monastery, and didn't we drink? The elder said: That eating was done out of charity, but let us keep our fast, son.[193]

---

[190] Julianus Pomerius, *De vita contemplativa*, 2.24; PL 59:470.

[191] The Latin *hospes* means both "guest" and "stranger."

[192] RB 53.1-2. The rest of this paragraph follows closely, with changes, RB 53.10-11, 15.

[193] *Vitae patrum*, 5.4.40; PL 73:870.

This account makes it clear that, if we exercise discretion, we can accomplish both goals, that is, at certain times we can eat for the sake of charity with guests who arrive, and yet not abandon the rule of fasting. Accordingly Saint Cassian asked a certain elder about this matter: "Why is it that among you the daily fast is indiscriminately broken for the sake of guests? The elder answered: My fast is always with me, but I will soon take leave of you and will not be able always to hold you, and so I fulfill the duty of charity toward you. And he added: The sons of the bridegroom cannot fast as long as the bridegroom is with them. But when he departs, then they will fast [see Matt 9:15]. So too, when we have taken leave of you, we will rightly observe the rule of our fasting."[194]

Chapter 56: Charity

Charity is love of God and neighbor with the whole heart and the whole mind. Charity holds the primacy among the other virtues, since without it no one has the power to ascend to the summit of perfection. Only then are we perfect, when we are full of charity, the charity that the Apostle commands us to have, when he says: "But above all things have charity, which is the bond of perfection" [Col 3:14], and also: "Loving one another in fraternal love" [Rom 12:10]. Thus the apostle Peter says: "Before all things, however, have constant charity among yourselves, because charity covers a multitude of sins" [1 Pet 4:8]. And the apostle John says: "God is charity, and all who abide in charity abide in God and God in them" [1 John 4:16]. For this reason, the unity of charity is to be maintained by all holy people, and especially by solitaries, since the more they withdraw from the world, the greater is their need to have love for God and neighbor. Only then will they be servants of the love of God, when they are not separated from the charity of their neighbor. That is why Truth himself says: "By this will everyone know that you are my disciples, if you have love for one another" [John 13:35].

---

[194] John Cassian, Inst. 5.24.1; PL 49:243–44. The last sentence of Grimlaicus' account is not found in Cassian. A version of this story occurs in *Vitae patrum*, 5.13.6; PL 73:944, but Grimlaicus' text is closer to that of Cassian.

The extent of the charity that our holy fathers had for one another is shown in the following example:

> Once a certain brother came to the holy Macarius and brought him, for charity's sake, a single grape. Macarius thanked God for the service the brother had rendered, and, acting in charity, he immediately brought it to another brother who seemed to be weaker than he. But this brother, thinking more about his neighbor than about himself, brought that same grape to another brother, and this brother in turn brought it to another, and this one brought it to still another. Thus that grape was carried around through all the cells that were scattered far and wide in the desert, and no one knew who had sent it in the first place. Macarius rejoiced to see among the brothers such charity and such self-control, and he exerted himself even more in the practices of the spiritual life.[195]

I believe that among those holy brothers there was perfect charity, because none of them sought what was his but what was another's. Indeed, such is the power of charity, as the Apostle testifies, that neither martyrdom nor contempt of the world, nor generosity in almsgiving is of any use without it [see 1 Cor 13:1-3]. Consequently, if we want to arrive safe and sound in our heavenly homeland, we must strive to have true charity for God and neighbor, because, just as no one can reach a destination without a road, so without charity, which is called the road, we cannot walk along but only go astray. Furthermore, all goodness comes from charity and from humility. Just as fire cannot exist without heat and light, so charity cannot exist without humility and true obedience. We must realize, however, that humility and obedience and the other virtues begin with the body and cease along with the body, even though the merit they win abides forever, but charity begins in the present age but abides with God in the age to come.

---

[195] *Vitae patrum*, 3.42; PL 73:765. Oddly, Grimlaicus' version omits the punch line of the story: finally, the grape found its way back to the one who had originally brought it.

Chapter 57: Humility

The Lord has deigned by own example to invite us to the summit of true humility. He says: "Learn from me for I am gentle and humble of heart, and you will find rest for your souls" [Matt 11:29], and the apostle Peter says: "Humble yourselves under the mighty hand of God, and he will exalt you" [1 Pet 5:6]. By this we are given to understand that the more we lower ourselves down to the depths for the love of Christ, the more we are advancing to the height, and the more glorious we appear in our pride among human beings, the more insignificant we will be before God. The Lord says the same thing in the words: "All who exalt themselves will be humbled, and those who humble themselves will be exalted" [Luke 14:11]. In saying this, he shows us that all exaltation is a kind of pride.[196] Since God became humble on account of our salvation, a human being should be ashamed to be proud, for, as Solomon says: "Where there was pride, there also will insult be, but where there was humility, there also will wisdom be" [Prov 11:2]. And upon such a person the Holy Spirit will rest, as the Lord says through the prophet: Upon whom will my Spirit rest, unless upon the one who is humble and quiet and who trembles at my words? [see Isa 66:2].

Consequently, if you are not humble and quiet, the grace of the Holy Spirit cannot dwell in you. If you hold to humility in your conduct, secret things are laid open to you and also whatever is hidden in the divine utterances. The conscience of solitaries ought always to be humble and sorrowful. Why? So that it not become proud through its humility and so that, by means of a beneficial sadness, the heart not become dissolute and turn to indecent pleasures.

Furthermore, through humility unclean spirits are made subject to God's servants, as we read in the conferences of the fathers: "A person who was being tormented by a demon and was frothing violently saw a certain elder who was a solitary. He raised his hand and struck him on the cheek, but the elder followed the Lord's

---

[196] See RB 7.1-2.

precept and turned to him the other. At once the demon could not stand being burned by the elder's humility. He screamed and wailed and left that person."[197]

Another time

> Abba Macarius was going through the desert, and there came up to him on the road a devil who had a reaper's sickle. The devil wanted to strike him with the sickle, but he couldn't. The demon said: I'm enduring great violence from you, O Macarius, because I can't prevail against you. Look, whatever you do, I also do. You fast, and I eat nothing; you keep vigil, and I don't sleep at all. But there's one thing in which you defeat me. And Abba Macarius said to him: What's that? And the devil responded: Your humility conquers me. Because of it I don't prevail against you.[198]

How great is the strength of humility! Not only does it save human beings, but it overcomes demons. Blessed Anthony showed how great was the strength of humility when he said: "I saw all the snares of Satan laid out on the ground, and I groaned and said: Who do you think will get across them? And I heard a voice saying to me: Humility."[199]

Therefore let us bend down the neck of our heart in true humility. Then we will be able to pass through all the snares of Satan unharmed. We will have true humility if, when others have sinned against us, we forgive them before they ask pardon. We have true humility if, when we have been hurt, we do not get angry and do not allow others to get angry, but rather pray for them from the heart.

Now if you are disposed to delve more deeply into humility, turn to the Rule of Saint Benedict. There you will find the twelve steps of humility very lucidly explained.[200]

---

[197] *Vitae patrum*, 5.15.53; PL 73:963.

[198] Ibid., 5.15.26; PL 73:959.

[199] Ibid., 5.15.3; PL 73:953. A similar saying is found in 3.129; PL 73:785.

[200] The steps of humility are found in RB 7.

Chapter 58: Obedience

Obedience is called compliance because a person humbly obeys or complies with the one who is commanding. They are rightly called obedient who, through the humility of obedience, submit themselves to God with their whole soul and in humility fulfill his precepts. They are also rightly called obedient who try, as much as their strength allows, humbly to fulfill the precepts of their master. Christ our Lord "committed no sin, and no deceit was found in his mouth" [1 Pet 2:22], yet he became for our sake obedient to the Father even unto death and thus left us an example that we should follow his footsteps [see Phil 2:8; 1 Pet 2:21].

Hence, the solitary should gladly comply with everything that the one commanding him tells him to do for the sake of religion. And if it should turn out that he is told to do onerous or impossible things, he should receive gladly and with all gentleness the order of the one issuing it. But if he realizes that what he is being told to do goes completely beyond his strength, he should not resist the order and repudiate it but humbly and patiently explain to the one who told him to do it why the thing is impossible, with a view to having the order modified.[201] Then what had been burdensome may be lightened, so that the sin of contradiction may be avoided.

Our holy fathers arrived at the summit of perfection by the labor of obedience. At this point we may insert the story of one among many who practiced marvelous obedience.

> A certain layman renounced the world; when he came to the monastery, he left three sons in the city. When he had spent three years in the monastery, his thoughts began often to call his sons to mind, and he used to become very sad on their account. When the abbot saw that he was sad, he said to him: What is the matter with you? Why are you sad? And he told him that he had three sons in the city and that he wanted to bring them to the monastery. The abbot ordered him to bring them. When he had reached the city, he discovered that two of his sons had already died and that there was only one left.

---

[201] Much of the foregoing paragraph depends on RB 68.

This son he took and brought to the monastery. The abbot
was in the bakery. When he saw him coming, he greeted him.
He took the infant whom the father was leading, hugged him
and kissed him. The abbot said to the father: Do you love him?
He answered: Yes. And again the abbot said to him: Do you
love him very much? And he answered: Yes. When the abbot
heard this, he said to him: If you love him, take him and throw
him into the oven right now while it is burning. And the father
took him and threw him into the burning oven. At once the
oven became like dew. Because of this, he received glory at
that time, just as the patriarch Abraham had.[202]

O what great obedience did that holy man have, who did not spare
his own son but, at the abbot's command, handed him over to the
flames [see Rom 8:32; Gen 22:16]! I think that, if the abbot had
ordered him for the sake of obedience to go into the oven, he
would have. But we have disobeyed the commands of God and of
his saints and also of our teachers and have withdrawn from God.
Yet let us through the labor of obedience return to the One who
said: "Come to me, all you who labor and are burdened, and I will
refresh you" [Matt 11:28].[203]

Chapter 59: The Virtue of Patience

True patience consists in steadfastly enduring injuries in the
present and not seeking revenge in the future but rather forgiving
from the heart the one who inflicts the injuries. For there are some
people who endure injuries patiently for a while, so that later they
can the more easily get revenge. Those people do not have true
patience. Really patient people love the ones they endure. To
tolerate while hating is not the virtue of gentleness but a veil for
rage. By patience we seek the virtue of gentleness and the ability
to forgive, not an opportunity to get revenge. Just as we ought to
suffer the injuries inflicted on us by others, so we have to suffer

[202] *Vitae patrum*, 5.14.18; PL 73:952.
[203] See RB Prol. 2.

patiently the afflictions of infirmities that happen to us. We are tested by God's scourges to show with what disposition[204] we act rightly and with what fortitude we suffer the temptations that come upon us. Hence the Apostle says: God is testing you to see if you love him [see Deut 13:3]. We know that testings come upon God's servants in three ways. First, they are tested by God through scourgings; second, by the devil through illusions and various stratagems; third, by their neighbor through injuries and abuse and persecutions. Blessed is the person who bears all of these patiently. About such a one Scripture says: "Blessed is the one who suffers testings," and the rest [Jas 1:12].

However, we can be martyrs without the sword if we truly maintain patience in our inner selves.[205] The less we display patience, the less we display learning. That is why it was said through Solomon: "Your learning is known by your patience" [Prov 19:11]. Above all, let us overcome with patience the abuse of those who speak wrongly about us. Let us break the arrows of abuse by the shield of patience. Let us hold up against the sword of the tongue the buckler of patience. And if people should inflict evil things on us, let us never become angry at them, but let us mourn for them instead, because God is angry at them.

Let us see how much patience that holy elder had about whom we will now speak.

> There was in the desert a certain great elder who lived by the labor of his hands. And there was another brother who was his neighbor and who used often to go in and steal what the elder had in his cell. Now the elder saw him and did not rebuke him but instead forced himself to work more than usual with his hands, saying: I believe he needs it. The elder tightened his stomach and ate scarcely enough bread. Now when that elder was dying, the brothers came and stood around him. He looked at the one who used to steal from him and said to him: Come here next to me. He took his hands and kissed them

---

[204] *quo animo*

[205] *in animo.* We are to be patient, not just in mind and thought, but also in heart and will.

and said: I give thanks to these hands, brother, since because
of them I am going to the kingdom of heaven. But that brother
was struck with remorse. He did penance and himself became
a proven monk and patterned himself on the actions of that
great elder.[206]

The patience of that holy monk is certainly praiseworthy, but
far more praiseworthy is the patience of Christ. That elder saw the
brother stealing and kept silence, but Christ endured insults, abuse,
mocking, slaps, spitting, whipping, the crown of thorns, and the
cross, and he did not speak an abusive word to anyone. That elder
gave thanks and kissed the hands of the thief, but Christ, fastened
to the cross, prayed for his persecutors. In all these things he left us
an example of patience. On account of this, let us make every effort
to be patient toward everyone and in everything, because, as Christ
says: "By your patience you will possess your souls" [Luke 21:19].
Let us be gentle, as the prophet says: "The gentle will inherit the
earth, and they will delight in abundance of bread" [Ps 36:11]. And
so if you are mild, gentle and patient, you are an imitator of God's
Son. And if you embrace peace in the guest room of your mind,
you are preparing in yourself a dwelling place for Christ, because
Christ is peace and is accustomed to take his rest in peace.

Chapter 60: Discretion

Discretion is the mother of all the virtues.[207] Hence in every
work, whether spiritual or bodily, solitaries should hold to the
proper measure dictated by discretion and not labor too hard and
so become weary in both heart and body. They should observe
due measure in all that they do, so that with ready will[208] they may
desire to exert themselves still more in good works. Whether it be
keeping vigil or fasting or abstinence or other similar things—they

---

[206] *Vitae patrum*, 5.16.19; PL 73:973.
[207] See RB 64.19.
[208] *alacri animo*

should do them in such a moderate way that their strength of spirit[209] not give up and their stamina of body not wear out.

About this a certain father used to say: "Our body is as fragile as a piece of clothing. If we take good care of it, it will last, but if we do not, it will fall apart in a short time."[210] Further:

> A certain man who was hunting wild animals in the forest came upon Abba Antony and saw him rejoicing with the brothers, and it displeased him. But the elder wanted to show him that sometimes one should indulge the brothers, and so he said to him: Please put an arrow in your bow and draw it. He did so. And he said to him again: Draw it. And he drew it. Draw it more, and he did so. The hunter said to him: If I draw it too much, the bow will break. Abba Antony said to him: It's the same with the works of God: if we strive too much, the brothers will quickly become tired. It's beneficial for a while to relax their rigor. When the hunter heard this, he was struck with remorse. He drew great profit from the word of the elder, and he departed. The brothers were strengthened, and then they went back to their place.[211]

Solitaries should keep these and other testimonies of discretion in mind. They should exercise such discernment and restraint in everything that they themselves may not give up because they are overly tired and that others do not run away from the journey they have begun.[212]

Chapter 61: Silence

Silence is the strength of humility and token of gravity, fosterer of virtues and guardian of souls. Thus Solomon says: "If you guard your mouth and tongue, you will guard your soul from difficulties"

---

[209] *animi virtus*

[210] This saying is the final lines of a longer apophthegm found in V*itae patrum*, 5.5.40; PL 73:886.

[211] V*itae patrum*, 5.10.2; PL 73:912.

[212] See RB 64.19.

[Prov 21:23]. Consequently, the more you restrain yourself by silence, the more you fix the point of compunction in heaven, and the more you bridle your tongue with the rein of silence, the more you lift your mind up to heavenly things.

That is why solitaries should love silence and keep their tongue from uttering anything bad or wicked or in any way foolish. They should say with the prophet: "I said: I will guard my ways so that I not offend with my tongue" [Ps 38:2], and also: "I have stationed a guard on my mouth" [Ps 38:2], and: "I said nothing and was humbled and kept silence from good things" [Ps 38:3].[213] You are guarding well your ways, that is, the actions of your life, if you commit no offense with your tongue. You are stationing a secure guard on your mouth if your tongue does not let forth an impudent stream of malicious, idle and incessant talk. To keep our tongue from falling into malicious speech, let us all guard our mouth and pay special attention to what the prophet says about those who speak wickedly: "May the Lord scatter all lying lips and the boastful tongue" [Ps 11:4]. And let us hear what Solomon says about the person who talks too much: "In talking too much you will not escape sin" [Prov 10:19], and: "They who use many words injure their soul" [Sir 20:8]. About this the prophet says: If you want to have true and everlasting life and desire to see good days, keep your tongue from evil, and do not let your lips speak deceit [see Ps 33:13-14]. And the Apostle says: "If people think they are religious and do not rein in their tongue but deceive their heart, their religion is worthless" [Jas 1:26].

Blessed Ambrose says: "Some people act as though they are keeping silence, but their hearts roundly condemn them. People of this sort are talking a great deal. But there are other people who speak from morning until evening but do it with discretion. These people are keeping great silence."[214] Now he was speaking about those who never speak except for the good of their hearers. A

---

[213] RB 6.1 also cites Ps 38:2-3 and Prov 10:19, quoted below by Grimlaicus. RB cites Ps 33:13-14 in Prol. 15-17.

[214] *Vitae patrum*, 5.10.51; PL 73-921, where the saying is attributed to Abba Pastor. Grimlaicus' wording is closer to the version found in Defensor, 16.39.

person is keeping silence well who does not speak until asked something. So then, solitaries should not go beyond the minimum in speech. There should always be measure in their words and balance in their speech. Their words should always be in moderation, and they should love listening more than speaking. They should not give an answer before they have listened. Thus it is written: "Those who give an answer before they have listened show that they are fools" [Prov 18:13].

As Saint Benedict says: Speaking and teaching befit the master; keeping silent and listening are proper for the disciple. And if anything must be requested of the master, the requests should be made with all humility and respectful submission. But vulgarity and useless chatter and jokes we condemn to be eternally barred in all places, and for that kind of talking we do not permit a disciple to open his mouth.[215]

Chapter 62: Avoiding Malicious Talk: Two Ways in Which Someone Can Speak about the Sins of Someone Else Without Sinning

Even though blessed Jerome says that "to tell the truth is not to malign,"[216] nonetheless solitaries must avoid maligning others at all cost, as blessed James the apostle warns: "My brothers and sisters, do not malign one another, for those who malign their brother or sister or who judge their brother or sister are maligning the Law and judging the Law" [Jas 4:11]. And Solomon says: "Remove from yourself a vicious mouth, and let malicious lips be far from you" [Prov 4:24], and also: "Do not associate with those who malign others, for suddenly their destruction will loom" [Prov 24:21-22]. Jerome has this to say: "Take care not to have an itching tongue or itching ears, that is, do not malign or listen to others who do,"[217] since the one who maligns and the one who willingly

---

[215] This paragraph is taken almost verbatim from RB 6.6-8.

[216] Jerome, Ep 117.1; PL 22:954. The saying, "Do not malign, but tell the truth," is found in Defensor, 51.

[217] Jerome, Ep 52.14; PL 22:538. This saying is also found in Defensor, 40.

listens to someone who is maligning have both committed the
same sin. About this Isidore says: "Do not malign a sinner but have
compassion. You must not malign something in another but rather
fear lest it be found in you."[218] And in the lives of the fathers it
says: "It is better to eat meat and drink wine every day than to tear
the flesh of the brothers by speaking disparagingly about them."[219]

Finally, as Saint Basil says:

> There are two ways in which we can speak about or recall the
> sins of others without maligning them. That is to say, it may
> sometimes be necessary to take counsel with others about
> how to correct someone who has sinned. In such an instance
> we can bring up that person's sins and speak openly about
> them without being malicious. Further, it may sometimes be
> necessary to deter and warn someone not to get involved with
> some bad person. In that case, we can, without maligning,
> reveal the sins of that other person. We find that the Apostle
> himself did this, for he says to Timothy: "Alexander the
> coppersmith did me great harm. You too should avoid him,
> for he has strongly resisted my preaching. God will repay him
> as his evil deeds deserve" [2 Tim 4:14-15]. Apart from these
> necessary instances, however, if you say something against
> another or deride or disparage that person, you are speaking
> maliciously, even if it seems that what you say is true.[220]

Chapter 63: Consolation of Solitaries in the Face of Malicious Talk

Solitaries should not become sad if, through no fault of theirs,
they are maligned by some spiteful people, since the Lord, in order

---

[218] Isidore of Seville, *Synonymorum Liber*, 2.50; PL 83:857. This saying is also
found in Defensor, 41. Grimlaicus' wording is closer the former.

[219] *Vitae patrum*, 3.134; PL 73:786 and also 5.4.51; PL 73:870. This saying is
also found in Defensor, 41. Grimlaicus' wording seems to be a combination of
that found in the versions in the *Vitae patrum*.

[220] Basil, *Regula*, 42, as found in the *Codex regularum*; PL 103:513. The same
passage also occurs in Benedict of Aniane's *Concordia regularum*, 7; PL 103:806.
Basil does not include 2 Tim 4:14b: "God will repay him as his evil deeds deserve."

to console us, deigned to point to the disgrace that he himself suffered, as he says: "If they called the father of the family Beelzebub, how much more his servants?" [Matt 10:25], and also: "If you were from the world, the world would love what belonged to it, but because you are not from the world, the world hates you" [John 15:19], and the Apostle says: "Do not be surprised if the world hates you" [1 John 3:13]. There are many who praise the life of solitaries perhaps more than they should. To keep them from being caught unawares by pride at such praise, almighty God allows bad people to burst upon them with disparaging remarks and scolding speech. And so, if any fault arises in the heart of solitaries because of what people say in their praise, solitaries may be recalled to penitence through the disparaging remarks of bad people. Yet in the midst of the words both of those who praise us and of those who censure us, we ought always to look within ourselves. If we do not find in ourselves the good that is being spoken about us, that should make us very sad. And if we do not find in ourselves the evil that people are speaking about us, we ought to break forth with great joy. Thus blessed Job says: "Behold my witness is in heaven, and my confidant is in the heights" [Job 16:20]. If you have in heaven the witness to your life, you should not fear the malicious speech of human beings, as Paul says: "Our glory is this: the testimony given by our conscience" [2 Cor 1:12]. If there were no people who were charging him with evil and calling him a seducer, he would not have said: "Famous and infamous, called seducers and truthful" [2 Cor 6:8]. And what are we to make of our Savior, whom the Jews called possessed by the devil and a blasphemer and a persecutor?

Blessed Arnulph, even though he was a bishop, later became a solitary. He bore with a quiet mind the malicious attacks of spiteful people. We read in the record of his acts: A certain man by the name of Noddo dared, along with his cohorts, to speak disparagingly about the blessed Arnulph. This Noddo said that he was no worshiper of God but rather a person given over to pleasure. Now when this slanderer had gone to bed with one of his fellow slanderers, God commanded that flames surround and envelop all their clothes. They dashed out from where they were and shouted for water, but the water that was thrown upon them did not extinguish the fire that God had sent. Their undergarments were burning fiercely around their genitals and buttocks, and they couldn't remove their burning garments. What else happened to them? Because they could do nothing else, they went running outside and, like pigs, they rolled around screaming in a muddy wallow. Even so, the fire that God had sent burned their genitals more and more. Then finally, I fear, what was written was fulfilled in them: "Those who malign a neighbor in secret, them will I persecute" [Ps 100:5]. God's judgment so ordered that they should experience in themselves the punishment for the things with which they had maligned the holy man. [221] But the holy bishop and solitary was neither saddened by malicious talk nor gladdened by the vindication God had brought him. No, as God had commanded, he loved them and prayed for them. By this example we too are taught not to be made sad by malicious talk but rather to rejoice in being slandered, remembering what is written: "The apostles went out rejoicing from the presence of the council, for they had deserved to suffer insult for the name of Jesus" [Acts 5:41]. If they were not made sad by slander and beatings, then we should not be made sad by words and malicious talk. What else are slanderers doing but blowing into the dust and stirring up dirt into their own eyes? They must be called and patiently reprimanded, as the Lord's command says: "If your brother sins against you, reprimand him. And if he says, I'm sorry, forgive him. And if he sins against you seven times a day and seven times says, I'm sorry, forgive him" [Luke 17:3-4]. Therefore if you do this, you will both save yourself and free from the pit of sin the neighbor who was maligning you.

Chapter 64: Thoughts and Diabolical Illusions

Just as solitaries ought to abstain from bad works and corrupt speech, so too should they guard their hearts against perverse thoughts. Blessed Jerome warns us about this when he says: "Do

---

[221] The narrative up to this point follows closely the *Sancti Arnolfi episcopi vita et miracula* as found in PL 95:734–35 and in MGH SS rer. Merov., 437. See note 11.

not allow bad thoughts to grow in your heart." [222] And elsewhere: "Choke off the beginning of the thought and other things will not overwhelm you. The body cannot be corrupted unless the spirit[223] has first been corrupted, and the flesh cannot do anything except what the spirit wills. Therefore first cleanse the spirit from perverse thoughts, and the flesh will not sin forever." [224]

Good thoughts always come from God, whereas bad thoughts sometimes come from ourselves and sometimes are stirred up by the devil's urging. The devil can deceive no one except someone who wants to give the devil willing consent. If we fight against the devil, he will flee from us, as blessed James the apostle says: "Resist the devil, and he will flee from you" [Jas 4:7].

On this theme we read in the conferences of the fathers:

> At one time blessed Macarius was living alone in a deserted place, and nearby there was another solitude in which many brothers were living. The elder saw Satan who was coming in human form and intending to go past his cell. The elder saw that he had on an old worn-out linen tunic, and there were vials hanging out through all the holes in it. The elder said to him: Where are you going? He answered: I'm going to pay the brothers a visit. The elder said: And why do you have those vials? He said: I'm bringing the brothers a taste. The elder said to him: These vials you are bringing, they all have a taste? He answered: Yes. If someone doesn't like one, I offer him another, and if he doesn't like that one, I offer him a third, and so on down the line. He's bound to like one of them. When he had said these things, he went on his way. The elder watched and kept his eye on the roads, until he returned. And when the elder saw him, he said to him: Health to you. And he answered:

[222] Jerome, Ep 22.6; PL 22:398. This saying also occurs in Defensor, 37. Grimlaicus' wording is closer to that of Defensor.

[223] The three occurrences of *animus* in this citation are all translated "spirit," but it should be kept in mind that the immediate context is different each time and that English might well use a different word for each occurrence: contrasted with *corpus*, "body," *animus* could mean "soul;" paired with *caro*, "flesh," it would tend to mean "spirit;" together with *a pravis cogitationibus*, "from perverse thoughts," it has the meaning "mind."

[224] Isidore of Seville, *Synonyma*, 2.7; PL 83:847

How can I be healthy? The elder said: What do you mean? He
answered: They've all achieved holiness by means of me, and
no one gives me his consent. And the elder said: Don't you have
any friends there? And he answered: I have only one brother
there, and he's the only one who gives me his consent. When
he sees me, he turns around like the wind. But the elder said
to him: What's that brother's name? He answered: Theoctistus.
And when he had said these things, he went his way. But Abba
Macarius got up and went to see the brothers. When they
heard that he was coming, they took palm branches and
hurried to meet him. Each one of them got his cell ready, since
they did not know which of them he would choose to stay
with. The elder inquired which of them was called Theoctistus,
and when he had found him, he went into his cell. And so
Theoctistus welcomed him joyfully. But when they had begun
to talk in private, the elder said to him: How are you doing,
brother? And he said: With the help of your prayers, I'm doing
well. And the elder said: Don't your thoughts harass you? He
answered again: I'm doing well. He was ashamed to tell him.
And the elder said to him: Look at how many years now I've
been living the life of a monk in this place, and everybody
honors me. Yet in my old age I'm plagued by a spirit of
fornication. And Theoctistus answered: Believe me, abba, I am
too. The elder pretended to be bothered by other thoughts
too, until he had the brother confess. Next he said: How do
you fast? And the brother said: Until the ninth hour. The elder
said to him: Fast until evening and abstain and read the gospels
so that you memorize them. And meditate on the other Scriptures from the heart,[225] and if a bad thought presents itself,
never glance downward but always upward, and immediately
the Lord will help you. When the elder had set the brother
straight, he went back to his solitude. And when he looked
up, he again saw that devil, and he said to him: Where are you
going now? And he answered: To visit the brothers. And he
went on his way. But when he came back, the elder said to him:
How are those brothers? He answered: Terrible. The elder
said: Why? And he answered: Because they're all holy, and

---

[225] *ex animo meditare scripturas.* Meditating, like reading, was practiced with the
voice as well as with the mind. The elder is telling the brother to speak the passages of Scripture over and over to himself so that he has them "by heart."

what's worse, the only one who was my friend and obeyed me, even he—I don't know how—has been turned against me. Now he doesn't give me his consent but has become holier than all the others, and so I've sworn not to set foot in that place for a long time. When he had said these things, he went on his way and left the elder. But the holy elder went into his cell worshiping and thanking God.²²⁶

From this account we learn that, unless a person voluntarily submits to the devil's wishes, he has no power over a human being. And as the account showed, Satan does not know by which passion the soul may be seduced. That is why he sows his weeds in it. Sometimes he sows the seeds of fornication; at other times those of malicious speech or of the other vices. He does the same with the passions, and to whichever passion he sees a person²²⁷ turn aside, that is the one he provides it with. Now nothing so frustrates the demon as when his stimuli are revealed, and nothing makes him so happy as when his thoughts are kept hidden. Since our Lord Jesus Christ gave us power to tread on snakes and scorpions, that is, bad thoughts, let us cleanse our hearts by humble confession and let us smash the little ones, our thoughts, against Christ, since what is written is said of us: "Blessed the one who will take and smash your little ones against the rock" [Ps 136:9],²²⁸ and also: "Blessed the clean of heart, for they will see God" [Matt 5:8].

Chapter 65: The Various Temptations of Solitaries

Thus we see that the minds of solitaries are buffeted by many destructive temptations in this life. Yet the devil does not tempt them beyond what God's will permits. By tempting them, the devil instructs them how to make progress. Even though he does not will it, nonetheless the devil acts for their benefit when by his temptations he does not ensnare but instruct them. As we have said,

---

²²⁶ *Vitae patrum*, 5.18.9; PL 73:981. It is also found in 3.61; PL 73:769, but Grimlaicus' version is closer to the former.

²²⁷ Here *animus* is virtually synonymous with *anima* several lines above. Both mean "a person's mind and will."

²²⁸ See RB Prol. 28 and 4.50.

the devil tempts the minds of solitaries in many ways. Sometimes he tempts them by the goad of poverty, and when he cannot move them by the goad of poverty, he uses wealth to seduce them. When he does not overcome them by slander and disgrace, he tries to use praise and honor. If he has no success with bodily health, he sends sickness. And if he cannot seduce them with pleasures, he attempts to overthrow them by afflictions that happen despite their prayer. He tries to use certain serious infirmities against those he is tempting; if he can make the solitaries cowardly by means of them, then he can disturb the love they have for the Lord.

But even though your body is going to wrack and ruin and is burning up with severe fevers and is being battered by unbearable torments besides, whoever you are who are undergoing these things, remember the punishments of the world to come and the eternal fire and endless torments. If you keep these in mind, you will not give way to what is happening to you in the present world. Indeed, rejoice because God has visited you, and keep on your tongue that most famous saying: "Punishing, the Lord has punished me and has not given me over to death" [Ps 117:18], and: "The one whom the Lord loves he disciplines; he chastises every child whom he accepts" [Heb 12:6]. If you are iron, you will get rid of rust once fire has been put to you. If you are just and endure these things, you are being summoned from great to even greater things. You are gold, but it is by means of fire that you will be more purified. Has an angel of Satan been given to you, a thorn in your flesh [see 2 Cor 12:7]? Rejoice, since you see whom you resemble: Paul the apostle, and you have deserved to receive a gift like his. Listen how the Apostle gloried in his weaknesses; you too glory and say: "Willingly therefore will I glory in my weaknesses, that the power of Christ may dwell in me" [2 Cor 12:9], and also: "When I am weak, it is then that I am strong" and powerful [2 Cor 12:10]. If you are being chastised by fevers or by the biting cold, remember what Scripture says: "We have gone through fire and water" [Ps 65:12]. It remains for you to be led out into refreshment [see Ps 65:12]. Cry out with the prophet: "In hardship you have expanded me" [Ps 4:2]. By means of hardships like these you will be perfect. If it happen that you lose your eyes, do not take it badly; you have lost an instrument of haughtiness [see Sir 23:5], but be eager to look upon the glory of God with interior eyes. Have you become deaf? Do not be sad, since the hearing you have lost is useless. Has some affliction made your hands lame? Hold your inward hands ready to counter the temptations of the enemy. Does sickness have a grip on your whole body? Then the health of the inner person is growing. For illness of the body is nothing else but health of the mind. If the sickness is such that you cannot stand up to pray and sing the psalms, do not be sad on that account, because your sickness is praying for you. If you are fasting, do not look for an excuse for yourself by saying: You have abused your health; that is why you have become sick. After all, even those who do not fast become sick too. Have you begun some good work? Do not be turned from it by the difficulties the enemy puts in your way. It has been determined that we should fast and labor on account of shameful pleasures. All these things help us to destroy the desires of the body.

It is good for the just person to be tempted, but with a temptation that causes pain, not that excites lust. Hence those who suffer evil should learn not to complain, even though they do not know why they are suffering evil. They should think that they are suffering it justly because they are being judged by the One whose judgments are never unjust. Those who complain when they are chastised are accusing the justice of the One who is judging, whereas those who rightly recognize that they are enduring sufferings sent by the just Judge, even though they do not know the reason for their suffering, are justified because they accuse themselves and praise God's justice. Blessed is the one who bears all these things patiently.

Chapter 66: The Temptations of Dreams

It often happens that demons rush upon solitaries at night. They terrify them and throw them into confusion while they are slumbering. Those whom they tempt interiorly while they are awake but do not overcome, these they attack furiously while they are asleep. Sometimes they launch an open attack and do violence to human bodies and beat them, as they did to blessed Anthony. God permits this to happen that it may result in the punishment of the wicked and the endurance and glory of the just. Very often the unclean spirits catch sight of some people bent on loving the world. When these people are asleep, the spirits fool them with some empty hope of prosperity. We read in the Book of the Dialogues that "this happened to a certain person. While his entire attention was fixed on his dreams, it was promised him in a dream that he would enjoy great longevity. While he was amassing a great deal of money to support himself during a very long life, he died suddenly and left all his money untouched, and he took with him no good works."[229]

Sometimes Satan transforms himself into an angel of light, not only while we are asleep, but even while we are awake, so that he may fool someone into believing a delusion. Thus we read in the conferences of the fathers about

> a certain elder who was sitting in his cell. As he was enduring temptations, he saw demons in plain sight, and he disdained them. But when the devil saw that he had been beaten by the elder, he came and showed himself to him and said: Do you want to see Christ? And the elder answered and said: I anathematize you and the one you are talking about. For my part, I believe in my Christ who said: "If anyone says to you: Behold, Christ is here, or he is there, do not believe it" [Matt 24:23]. And the devil said: I am Christ. When the elder saw him, he closed his eyes. And the devil said to him: Why have you closed your eyes? The elder said: I don't want to see Christ here. I want to see him in the blessed life. When he heard these words, the devil left him.[230]

This account shows how many stratagems the enemy uses to try to deceive God's servants. But those who are aware of having committed either no or few transgressions or who are never or rarely

---

[229] Gregory the Great, *Liber dialogorum*, 4.49; PL 77:412.

[230] The incident, as Grimlaicus has it, is found in two items in the V*itae patrum*: 5.15.70 and 71; PL 73:965–66. The center portion, from "Do you want to see Christ?" up to "Do not believe it" is from 71; the beginning and ending portions are 70.

tormented by nocturnal terrors, even if they are thrown off balance at the moment of the temptation, soon wake up and spurn these hollow illusions and turn to focus their attention on God.

Now it sometimes happens that God's servants see certain hidden and mystic things in visions. Sinners, on the contrary, who pollute their hearts with serious sins, are misled by the fear inspired by their conscience and see terrifying sights. While such people are awake, the devil drags them toward sins, and while they are asleep, he tires them out and never lets them get any rest. In the eyes of sinners the devil is terrifying; in the eyes of the just the devil's terror is puny.

It should be noted that there are various kinds of dreams. Sometimes dreams arise because the stomach is full or is empty. Sometimes they come from thoughts, as it is written: "Dreams follow many worries" [Eccl 5:2]. It often happens that what we think about during the day we call to mind during the night. Sometimes dreams arise from the illusion caused by unclean spirits, as Solomon says: "Dreams and empty illusions make many people go astray" [Sir 34:7]. And sometimes dreams come from revelation, as we read in the Law concerning Joseph, the son of Jacob, who foretold by a dream that he would be set over his brothers [see Gen 37:5-8]. In the gospel it says that Joseph, the spouse of blessed Mary, was warned in a dream that he should flee with the child into Egypt [see Matt 2:13]. Sometimes, to be sure, dreams are produced from revelation and from thought at the same time, as Daniel says: "You, O king, began to ponder on your bed what would happen after these things, and the One who reveals mysteries is showing you what is coming" [Dan 2:29]. The better to deceive people, the demons often foretell many true things, so that in the end they can deceive or ensnare the soul with some lie. But even though some dreams may be true, still it is best not to believe them, for fear that sometimes they arise from the devil's illusion and may deceive the hearts of simple people. We should recall the testimony of Scripture that says: If they tell you and it happens, do not believe [see Deut 13:2-5; Matt 24:23-28]. Dreams are like omens, and those who pay attention to them are in fact really interpreting omens. For their part, solitaries should use discretion and circumspection in discerning between illusions and revelations and in this way come to know what they are receiving from the good Spirit and what they are suffering from the evil spirit.

Chapter 67: Solitaries Should Not Seek to Perform Signs and Miracles

Solitaries should not seek signs and miracles, because of the danger of showing off and of vainglory. Those who want to show their worth by the tokens of signs and miracles will turn out to be worth nothing.[231] Our Lord and Savior did not say: By signs and miracles will you know them, but: "By their fruits will you know them" [Matt 7:20]. Likewise, he did not promise that on the day of judgment he would reward those who worked signs and miracles but rather those who obeyed his precepts. He will say to them: "Come, blessed of my Father; take possession of the kingdom," and so on [Matt 25:34]. He called blessed, not those who worked signs and miracles, but those who were humble in spirit and gentle, who mourned and who performed works like that. Blessedness is not to be found in working signs but in carrying out God's commandments. It is a good life and worthy deeds, even without signs and miracles, that deserve a crown, but a wicked way of life,[232] even though it work signs and wonders, does not avoid punishment. Consequently, it is useless to seek signs and miracles. In fact, it is dangerous.

Solitaries should not do anything for show. Here is an example that demonstrates how much evil comes from doing something for show.

> There once was a young monk who saw some elders making a journey, and, just to show off, he commanded wild-asses to come and carry them until they arrived home. Now those elders told this to blessed Anthony. And Abba Anthony said: It seems to me that that monk is like a ship loaded with every

---

[231] Grimlaicus plays on the words *probari* and *probus*: *quisquis signorum et mirabilium indiciis vult probari, non potest probus videri.*

[232] *iniqua conversatio*

good thing, but it is uncertain whether or not it can reach port. A short time later Abba Anthony suddenly began to weep and to pull his hair and to mourn. When his disciples saw this, they said: Why are you crying, abba? He answered: A great pillar of the church has just fallen. He was speaking about that young monk. Go to him, brothers, he said, and see what he is doing. And so his disciples went off and found that monk sitting and bewailing a sin he had committed. When he saw the elder's disciples, he said to them: Tell the elder to beg God to give me just ten days reprieve. He died five days later.[233]

That is the reason why solitaries should take care not to do anything for show. Furthermore, they should flee the disease of vainglory that strikes solitaries, not only in carnal sins, but also in spiritual cases. For those who cannot be deceived by carnal sins are more seriously wounded by spiritual ones that come after. Someone whom the devil cannot plunge into vainglory by the outward appearance of expensive and sleek clothes he tries to deceive by clothing that is filthy and unkempt. And someone he cannot overthrow by honor he vanquishes by humility, and someone he is unable to raise up by the embellishment of knowledge and fine speech he crushes down by the gravity of silence. If someone fasts publicly, that person is struck by the vanity of becoming famous. If someone hides the fasting in order to spurn vainglory, that person tumbles into the same sin of self-exaltation. One person is struck by prayer, another by lengthy vigils. Many people, in trying to flee from vainglory, fall right into it. Many people want to be praised for despising praises, and, by an incredible inversion, seek praise even while they are avoiding it. That is why our holy fathers "use an apt image to describe this vice: an onion. Take off one layer of skin and you find it is covered by another. As often as one skin is peeled off, it is still covered by another."[234] Consequently solitaries should follow the Apostle's advice and go forward "with the weapons of justice on right hand and on left" [2 Cor 6:7] and continue on through glory and ignominy, through infamy and good reputation.

[233] *Vitae patrum*, 5.8.1; PL 73:905.
[234] John Cassian, *De institutis coenobiorum* 11.5; PL 49:404.

As is said through Solomon: They should turn aside neither to right nor to left [see Prov 4:27], in other words, they should neither exalt themselves because of the virtues and "right-hand" successes nor bend to the path of "left-hand" vices. Rather they should keep to the middle, to the One who is the Way, the Truth, and the Life and walk along so successfully that they deserve to reach their goal.

Chapter 68: The Threefold Grace of Charisms

The foregoing discussion has brought us to the point where we can relate what we have to say about spiritual charisms. The tradition of our elders has taught us that these charisms are threefold.

The first instance of cures is when the grace of signs attends certain holy and just people because of the merit of their holiness. For example, it is well known that the apostles and many holy people worked signs and wonders by the authority of the Lord, who said: "Cure the sick, raise up the dead, cleanse lepers, cast out demons. You have received at no cost; give at no cost" [Matt 10:8].

The second instance is when, in order to build up the faith either of the church or of those who bring sick people or of those who are to be cured, health-giving strength goes forth even from sinners and unworthy people. About these people the Lord says in the gospel: "On that day many will say to me: Lord, Lord, didn't we prophesy in your name, cast out demons, and work many miracles? And then I will declare to them: I do not know you. Depart from me, you workers of iniquity" [Matt 7:22-23]. And that is why he warns his disciples: "Do not rejoice because the demons have been made subject to you but because your names have been written in heaven" [Luke 10:20].

The third kind of cure is even simulated with the collusion and collaboration of demons. Despite the fact that someone is guilty of public offenses, still, because of the wonder aroused by the signs, that person is thought to be a saint and God's servant. It is certain that people who think that they have graces for curing and who are exalted in the pride of their own heart will be severely crushed. That is why the Lord says in the gospel: "Pseudo-Christs will arise, and pseudo-prophets, and they will work great signs and wonders,

so that, were it possible, even the chosen would be led into error"
[Mark 13:22].

Consequently people should be praiseworthy among us, not
because we admire the signs they work but because they adorn
their conduct with virtue. Truly, it is a greater miracle to eliminate
the kindling of lust from one's own flesh than to expel unclean
spirits from other people's bodies. And it is a more wonderful sign
to restrain the combative stirrings of anger by the virtue of patience
than to command demons or drive sicknesses out of other people's
bodies. And it is a more excellent virtue to cure the feebleness of
one's own soul than that of someone else's body.

The higher a soul is above the flesh, the closer is its salvation.
And there is greater merit in raising a sinner from vice than a dead
person from the tomb. That is why we never read that the holy
fathers ever aspired to work signs. On the contrary, even though
they possessed the ability to work such signs by the power of the
Holy Spirit, they never wanted to exercise it, except perhaps when
unavoidable necessity forced them to do so, as it did blessed
Macarius, who was a disciple of Saint Anthony. They say that once,

> when there had been a murder in a nearby place, an innocent
> man had been charged with the murder. The one who had
> been wrongly accused had fled to Macarius' cell. There were
> also people present who were denouncing the innocent man.
> They swore and said that they were endangering themselves
> unless they apprehended the murderer and brought him to
> justice. The man who stood accused of the crime swore with
> oaths that he was not guilty of that blood. When this battle
> had been going on for a long while, Saint Macarius asked
> where the presumed victim was lying. When they had pointed
> out the place, he went to the tomb with all those who had
> come to denounce the man. There he knelt down and invoked
> the name of Christ. He said to those present: Now the Lord
> will show if this man you are denouncing is guilty. He raised
> his voice and called the dead man by name. When he answered
> him from the tomb, he said to him: By faith in Christ I adjure
> you to say if you were killed by the one who is being accused
> because of you. Then the dead man raised his voice and answered

from the tomb that he had not been harmed by him. When they all heard this, they were stupefied and fell to the ground. Prostrate at his feet, they begged him to ask the dead man who had killed him. He responded: That I won't ask. It's enough for me that an innocent man is set free. It is not for me to hand over the guilty one.[235]

We see that no one would ever have known how much power and grace was in him, unless the need of a person in danger and a sincere love for Christ had forced him to work this miracle. We should realize that, just as a treasure out in the open is quickly spent, so too any power, if it is public, will be eradicated. And just as wax melts when it is put near fire, so too a soul that is lifted up by empty praises loses the strength of its powers. That is why solitaries, if they are aware of some good work in themselves, need to hide it, and when they have done everything that God commands, they should say: "We are useless servants" [Luke 17:10]. It is the same with powers: if they sense that they have powers in them, they should keep quiet and conceal them. God will disclose their works and make them known to everyone when the Lord comes "who will bring to light things hidden in darkness and will make public the counsels of hearts, and then each one will have praise from God" [1 Cor 4:5]. Then he will repay all individually as their works deserve.

Chapter 69: Solitaries, After They Have Been Enclosed, Must Never Return to Secular Life, and Perseverance in Good Works

Once solitaries have been enclosed, it is completely contrary to ecclesiastical rules that, whether because of pride or because of worldly affairs, they be so unfortunate as to return to the world and thus become the prey of demons. In the Gospel the Lord testifies how grave an offense it is for solitaries to become apostate, that is, to go back on their previous resolve: "No one who puts a hand

[235] *Vitae patrum*, 3.41; PL 73:764.

to the plow and then looks back is fit for the reign of God" [Luke 9:62], and Paul the Apostle says: "No one who is a soldier for God gets involved in secular affairs, so that he may please the one who enlisted him" [2 Tim 2:4]. They are not free from the snares of the devil who, after having been enclosed, want to get tangled up in worldly affairs. It is to such people that the true and terrifying statement of blessed Peter applies: "It would have been better for that person never to have recognized the way of life[236] than to have recognized it and then turned back" [2 Pet 2:21], and also: "The dog went back to its own vomit, and the sow was washed but is in the mud wallow" [2 Pet 2:22].

Therefore, those who succumb to the devil's persuasion and attempt to act in this way, unless forced to do so by unavoidable necessity, should by all means be excommunicated by their bishop or by other prelates, until such time as they return to their former resolve that, for God's sake, they had originally chosen. After all, it is not the beginning of good work that is looked for in solitaries but the end, because it is on how we end that each of us will be judged, not on how we have previously lived. Thus the Lord says through the prophet: I will judge you on the kind of person I have found you to be [see Ezek 7:3].

What is worse, there are those who begin their consecrated way of life[237] well but end it badly, like Judas, who started out well but finished badly, whereas Paul started out badly but finished well. Many people start out, but it is the rare person who reaches the peak of perfection. That is why the prize is not promised to those just beginning[238] but is given to those who persevere, as the Lord says: "It is the one who perseveres to the end who will be saved" [Matt 10:22].

---

[236] The Vulgate text has *non cognoscere viam justitiae*, "not known the way of justice," whereas our text reads *viam vitae non agnoscere*.

[237] *conversationem.* The context shows that *conversatio* here refers, not to a manner of life in general, but to a specifically monastic or consecrated way of life.

[238] The text has here *insipientibus*, "to those who are foolish, unwise." This word might be interpreted as "inexperienced," but more probably it is an error for *incipientibus*, "those who are starting out." (See RB Prol. 48.)

But if you, a solitary, think that you are so secure that you can now and then leave the solitary life because you have been running well on the road of your resolve and have worked very hard at it, you are acting like someone who weighs anchor and sails a ship laden with cargo out of port and who lets a storm take it and then steers it onto reefs and rocks. If you are thinking like that, you should see how uncertain and how slippery are the ways that human beings depart this life, as is said through Solomon: "People do not know whether they are deserving of love or of hate, but all things are kept uncertain in the future" [Eccl 9:1-2].

Consequently, no one should be secure about the past, because even though the manner of life of solitaries[239] be commendable, nevertheless, human beings remain unsure for what end they have been destined. Their starting out will be happy and blessed, their manner of life[240] will be pleasing to God, only if they avoid every shipwreck of error and wavering and arrive safe and sound at their chosen end and perfection.

Consequently, solitaries should be diligent in reading and assiduous in meditating on this rule that has been gathered in a few words from the flowers of the Holy Scriptures and strengthened here and there by the examples of the holy fathers. They should go through it word by word and commit it to memory and with the help of God's grace live it out as far as they are able. Then they will be able to arrive at the glory that eye has not seen nor ear heard nor has it entered into the human heart, the glory that God has prepared for those who love him [see 1 Cor 2:9], with the help of the One who lives and reigns, God, through all ages of ages. Amen.

---

[239] *solitariorum conversatio*
[240] *eorum conversatio*

Index of Scriptural References

"See" indicates that a passage is referred to but not quoted exactly. The number(s) on the right give the chapter of the Rule in which the scriptural citation is found.

Index of Patristic and Monastic Authors

The chapter number of the rule follows the name of the work cited. Superscript numbers indicate the number of times the work is referenced in that chapter. The exact portion of a work used by Grimlaicus can be found in the notes for the text of the chapter.

Gregory the Great: *Dialogorum libri*, 36², 48, 66
————: *Homiliae in Hiezechihelem*, 21²
————: *Moralia in Hiob*, Prol, 20
————: *XL Homiliae in evangelia*, 4, 26, 30, 49²
————: *Regula pastoralis*, 22, 44
Gregory the Great (pseudo): *Epistula*, 37

Isidore of Seville: *De ecclesiasticis officiis*, 16
————: *Regula monachorum*, 49
————: *Sententiarum libri*, 22, 54
————: *Synonymorum liber*, 62, 64

Jerome: *Commentarium in evangelium Matthaei*, 3, 5, 7
————: *Commentarium in Ezechielem*, 24
————: *Epistulae*, 6, 16, 21, 26, 43, 46, 49, 54, 62², 64
————: *Vita sancti Pauli primi eremitae*, 1
Julianus Pomerius: *De vita contemplativa*, 5, 6, 41⁴, 55

Paul the Deacon (attrib.): *Sancti Arnolfi episcopi vita et miracula*, 1, 63
Prosper of Aquitaine: *Epigrammatum ex sententiis S. Augustini*, 36

Rufinus: *Historia monachorum*, 36, 51

Sancti Arnolfi episcopi vita et miracula, 1, 63
Sedulius Scotus: *Collectaneum miscellaneum*, 46²

Vitae patrum: liber 3.33, 56, 62, 68
————: *liber* 5.6², 7, 14⁶, 30, 32, 35, 39, 44, 47, 52, 54, 55, 57³, 58, 59, 60², 61, 62, 64, 66, 67
————: *liber* 6.31, 54

Index of Citations from the
Rule of Saint Benedict

On the left is the number of the RB chapter and verse, used by de Vogüe and Neufville and subsequent editions. On the right is the number of Grimlaicus' chapter(s).

Works Cited

The following works are cited by the translator in the introduction or notes. The patristic and monastic works cited in the text of the rule are listed in the Index of Patristic and Monastic Authors.

Benedict of Nursia. *Benedict's Rule: A Translation and Commentary.* Edited and translated by Terrence Kardong. Collegeville, MN: Liturgical Press, 1996.

―――. *Règle de Saint Benoît.* Edited and translated by Adalbert de Vogüé and Jean Neufville. SCh 181–86. Paris: Les Éditions du Cerf, 1971–72.

―――. *Rule of Saint Benedict.* Edited and translated by Justin McCann. London: Burns & Oates, 1952.

―――. *Rule of Saint Benedict 1980.* Edited and translated by Timothy Fry et al. Collegeville, MN: Liturgical Press, 1981.

Chartier, Marie-Christine. "*Reclus - En Occident.*" In *Dictionnaire de spiritualité acétique et mystique.* Edited by M. Viller et al., vol. 13, cols. 227–28. Paris: Beauchesne, 1988.

"*Concilium Veneticum.*" In *Concilia Galliae.* Edited by Charles Munier. CC vol. 148. Brepols: Turnhout, 1963. 150–57.

Constable, Giles. Intro. to *Apologia de barbis* of Burchhardt of Bellevaux. In *Apologiae duae*, ed. R. B. C. Huygens, CCCM, vol. 42, 46–150. Brepols: Turnhout, 1985.

Doerr, Otmar. *Das Institut der Inclusen in Süddeutschland. Beiträge zur Geschichte des alten Mönchtums und des Benedictinerordens* 18. Münster: Aschendorff, 1934.

Frank, Karl Suso. "Grimlaicus, 'Regula solitariorum.'" In *Vita Religiosa im Mittelalter: Festschrift für Kaspar Elm*, ed. F. J. Felten and N. Jaspert, 21–35. Berlin: Duncker & Humbolt, 1999.

Gougaud, L., OSB. "*Étude sur la réclusion religieuse.*" *Revue Mabillon* 13 (1923): 26–39 and 77–102.

Grégoire, Réginald, "*Grimlaic.*" In *Dictionnaire de spiritualité acétique et mystique*. M. Viller et al., vol. 6, cols. 1042–43. Paris: Beauchesne, 1967.

Gregory of Tours. *Historiae eccleciasticae Francorum libri decem*. PL 71:161–572.

———. *Liber de gloria beatorum confessorum*. PL 71:827–910.

———. *Vitae patrum*. PL 71:1009–96.

Gregory the Great. *Moralia in Hiob (Morales sur Job)*. Ed. R. Gillet, O.S.B. Trans. A de Gaudemans, O.S.B. SCh 32bis. Cerf: Paris, 1975.

Grimlaici presbyteri regula solitariorum. In *Codex Regularum Monasticarum et Canonicarum*. Edited by Lucas Holstenius, vol. 1. Critico-historical notes by Marianus Brockie. Augsburg: Adam & Veith, 1759, pp. 291–344. (1957 repr. Akademische Druck- und Verlagsanstalt: Vienna). Reprinted in PL 103:574–664.

H. Leclercq. "*Reclus.*" In *Dictionnaire d'archéologie chrétienne*. Vol. 14 ii, cols. 2149–59. Paris: Letouzey, 1948.

Otfrid von Weißenburg. *Otfrids Evangelienbuch*. Edited by Oskar Erdmann and Edward Schröder. 5th ed. (with Ludwig Wolff). *Altdeutsche Textbibliothek* 49. Tübingen: Niemeyer, 1965.

Vita patrum Iurensium Romani, Lupicini, Eugendi. In *Passiones vitaeque sanctorum aevi merovingici*. Edited by Bruno Krusch. *MGH Scriptorum rerum merovingicarum*, vol. 3. Hannover: Hahn, 1896. Repr. 1977.

Vollmann, Benedikt. "*Gregor IV (Gregor von Tours).*" In *Reallexikon für Antike und Christentum*. Edited by Theodor Klauser et al. Stuttgart: Anton Hiersemann, 1981.